Bridging the Divide

Bridging the Divide

Anurag Anurag

Contents

1

International Intervention

International intervention can play a crucial role in facilitating, mediating, and enforcing a peace agreement between Israel and Palestine. Given the complexity and long-standing nature of the conflict, involving international actors provides an external framework that can help both sides navigate the challenges of reaching and maintaining a peace agreement. This approach aims to bring in a neutral, authoritative presence that ensures agreements are respected and both parties are held accountable to their commitments.

One of the primary tools of international intervention is the deployment of peacekeeping forces under the auspices of the United Nations or NATO. These forces would monitor ceasefire lines, prevent violence, and ensure that any breaches of the peace agreement are addressed promptly and impartially. The presence of international peacekeepers could provide both Israelis and Palestinians with a sense of security, knowing that a neutral third party is overseeing the situation. This could help to build trust between the two sides, reducing the likelihood of unilateral actions that might derail the peace process. Additionally, peacekeepers would maintain public order in sensitive areas, such as Jerusalem, and protect civilians from potential violence.

International intervention can also involve offering economic incentives to encourage both parties to commit to the peace process. These incentives could take various forms, including financial aid, development projects, trade agreements, and investments in infrastructure. The idea is to create a positive economic environment that makes peace more attractive than conflict. For example, international donors could fund infrastructure projects that benefit both Israelis and Palestinians, such as improving water and energy systems or building transportation networks that connect the two states. These projects would not only improve living conditions but also create economic interdependence, making it in both parties' interest to maintain peace. Moreover, trade agreements with major global economies could be contingent on the successful implementation of the peace agreement, providing a strong economic incentive for both sides to adhere to their commitments.

Diplomatic pressure is another essential component of international intervention. The global community, particularly influential powers like the United States, the European Union, and regional actors such as Egypt and Jordan, can use their diplomatic leverage to push both sides toward a resolution. This pressure can take various forms, from behind-the-scenes negotiations to public statements and sanctions. For instance, the international community could condition diplomatic recognition or economic aid on progress in the peace talks. Additionally, global institutions like the UN Security Council could pass resolutions that outline the parameters of the peace agreement and call on both sides to comply. The threat of international sanctions or isolation could serve as a powerful motivator for both Israel and Palestine to engage seriously in the peace process.

Beyond the initial deployment of peacekeeping forces and the application of economic incentives and diplomatic pressure, long-term international involvement may be necessary to monitor the implementation of the peace agreement and ensure that both sides adhere to their commitments. This could involve creating an international monitoring body, composed of representatives from the UN, regional organizations, and other key stakeholders. This body would be responsible for regularly assessing the progress of the peace process, identifying any violations of the agreement, and recommending corrective actions. In cases where violations occur, the monitoring body could work with the international community to impose sanctions or other penalties, ensuring that there are consequences for non-compliance. The goal of this monitoring and enforcement mechanism would be to maintain the momentum of the peace process and prevent backsliding while also providing a forum for addressing any new issues or disputes that arise during the implementation phase.

In addition to global powers, regional actors such as Egypt, Jordan, Saudi Arabia, and Turkey have a critical role to play in supporting international intervention efforts. These countries have significant influence over the dynamics of the Israel-Palestine conflict and can act as mediators, facilitators, or guarantors of the peace process. For example, Egypt and Jordan, which have peace treaties with Israel, could use their diplomatic channels to encourage Israeli cooperation, while also engaging with Palestinian leaders to ensure their interests are represented. Saudi Arabia, through its leadership in the Arab League, could help to build broader Arab support for the peace agreement, while Turkey could offer its services as a mediator, given its historical ties to the region. Regional actors could also contribute to the economic incentives by providing financial aid, investment, and technical expertise, particularly in areas where they have a comparative advantage, such as energy development or infrastructure projects.

While international intervention offers a powerful tool for advancing the peace process, it is not without its challenges. One of the key considerations is ensuring that the intervention is perceived as legitimate and neutral by both Israelis and Palestinians. This requires careful diplomacy, transparent communication, and a commitment to respecting the sovereignty and interests of both parties. Additionally, the international community must be prepared for the possibility that the peace process could be protracted and require sustained involvement over many years. This means securing long-term commitments from peacekeeping forces, financial donors, and diplomatic actors, and ensuring that the resources and political will are available to support the process until its successful conclusion.

Another challenge is the potential for external actors to become too deeply involved in the internal politics of Israel and Palestine, which could lead to unintended consequences or resentment from local populations. To mitigate this risk, international intervention should be designed to support, rather than dictate, the peace process, empowering Israeli and Palestinian leaders to take ownership of the agreement and its implementation. The ultimate goal of international intervention should be to create the conditions for a sustainable peace that can be maintained by the parties themselves, without the need for ongoing external involvement.

International intervention offers a comprehensive and multidimensional approach to resolving the Israel-Palestine conflict by combining security guarantees, economic incentives, and diplomatic pressure with robust monitoring and enforcement mechanisms. While the challenges are significant, the potential benefits of a successful international intervention—namely, a lasting and just peace in one of the world's most volatile regions—make it an option worth pursuing. By working together, the international community can help to bridge the gaps between Israelis and Palestinians, providing the support and oversight needed to transform a peace agreement from a fragile truce into a durable and resilient foundation for the future.

For international intervention to be effective in the Israel-Palestine conflict, it is essential that all actions and initiatives are well-coordinated and aligned with the broader goals of achieving a lasting peace. This requires a multi-layered strategy that not only addresses immediate security concerns but also builds the foundation for long-term stability and prosperity in the region. A crucial aspect of this strategy is the establishment of clear and measurable benchmarks that both Israel and Palestine must meet as part of the peace process. These benchmarks could include specific steps such as the dismantling of certain settlements, the withdrawal of military forces from key areas, the creation of joint security arrangements, or the implementation of economic development projects. The international community would play a key role in monitoring progress against these benchmarks and providing the necessary support to ensure they are met.

The success of international intervention also depends on the ability to engage with and include the broader populations of both Israel and Palestine. Peace agreements negotiated solely at the leadership level can falter if they do not have the buy-in of the people they are meant to benefit. Therefore, it is important to involve civil society organizations, community leaders, and grassroots movements in the peace process. These groups can help to communicate the benefits of peace to their communities, address concerns, and foster a culture of reconciliation and coexistence. International actors can support these efforts by providing funding, training, and platforms for dialogue, ensuring that the peace process is not only top-down but also bottom-up.

Moreover, international intervention should take into account the regional dynamics that influence the Israel-Palestine conflict. The Middle East is a region with complex political, religious, and economic interconnections, and developments in one area can have significant repercussions elsewhere. For instance, the role of Iran, with its support for groups like Hezbollah and its influence in Syria, must be carefully managed to prevent it from undermining the peace process. Similarly, the ongoing tensions in Lebanon, the situation in Iraq, and the broader Sunni-Shia divide in the region all have the potential to impact the stability of a future peace agreement between Israel and Palestine. As such, international intervention should be coordinated with broader regional efforts to promote stability and cooperation in the Middle East, potentially linking the Israel-Palestine peace process with other diplomatic initiatives in the region.

In addition to the direct benefits of achieving peace between Israel and Palestine, successful international intervention could also have positive ripple effects throughout the Middle East and beyond. A stable and peaceful Israel-Palestine could serve as a model for resolving other protracted conflicts, demonstrating that even the most deeply entrenched disputes can be resolved through diplomacy, cooperation, and international support. Furthermore, the economic benefits of peace—such as increased trade, tourism, and investment—could extend beyond Israel and Palestine to benefit the wider region, fostering greater economic integration and development.

However, the risks of failure must also be acknowledged. If international intervention is perceived as biased, ineffective, or overly intrusive, it could lead to a backlash from either or both parties, potentially escalating tensions rather than reducing them. Similarly, if the peace process stalls or collapses, it could result in a return to violence, with severe consequences for the region and the broader international community. Therefore, it is crucial that international intervention is carefully planned, transparent, and sensitive to the needs and concerns of both Israelis and Palestinians.

While international intervention is not a panacea for the Israel-Palestine conflict, it offers a vital means of supporting and sustaining the peace process. By deploying peacekeeping forces, providing economic incentives, applying diplomatic pressure, and engaging with regional and civil society actors, the international community can help to create the conditions necessary for a lasting and just peace. The challenges are significant, but the potential rewards—a stable, peaceful, and prosperous Middle East—make the effort worthwhile. If executed with care, commitment, and cooperation, international intervention could be the key to transforming the Israel-Palestine conflict from a seemingly intractable problem into a resolved issue that benefits not only the people directly involved but also the global community as a whole.

2

Introduction

The Israel-Palestine conflict stands as one of the most enduring and intractable disputes of the modern era, with deep historical roots, profound religious significance, and a seemingly endless cycle of violence and retaliation. For decades, this conflict has captured global attention, driven by a complex web of political, cultural, and emotional factors that make it uniquely challenging to resolve. The stakes are extraordinarily high: the conflict has led to untold suffering, displacement, and loss of life on both sides, and its resolution is critical not only for the people of Israel and Palestine but also for regional stability and global peace.

This book is an earnest attempt to navigate the complexities of the Israel-Palestine conflict and to explore viable pathways toward a just and lasting resolution. It is not merely a historical account or a political analysis; it is a call to action, aimed at identifying and evaluating the most promising solutions that could finally bring peace to this troubled region. At the heart of this exploration lies the recognition that both Israelis and Palestinians have legitimate claims, fears, and aspirations, and that any sustainable solution must address these concerns in a balanced and equitable manner.

The primary focus of this book is on the Two-State Solution, which has long been advocated as the most practical and fair resolution to the conflict. By establishing an independent Palestinian state alongside Israel, this solution seeks to fulfill the national aspirations of both peoples, allowing them to live side by side in peace and security. However, the path to achieving this vision is fraught with obstacles, including disputes over borders, the status of Jerusalem, the rights of refugees, and security arrangements. In the chapters that follow, we will delve deeply into these issues, examining the historical context, the key challenges, and the potential compromises that could make the Two-State Solution a reality.

In addition to the Two-State Solution, this book will explore other possible resolutions, such as the One-State Solution, confederation models, and various proposals for international intervention. Each of these alternatives offers different advantages and drawbacks, and understanding them is essential for anyone seeking to grasp the full range of possibilities for peace. The goal is not to advocate for a single solution but to present a comprehensive analysis of the options available, so that readers can form their own informed opinions.

This book is written for anyone who cares deeply about the future of Israel and Palestine, whether they are directly affected by the conflict, engaged in diplomatic or peace-building efforts, or simply concerned citizens of the world. It is intended to be both a resource for understanding the complexities of the conflict and a guide for thinking critically about the paths to peace. By engaging with the ideas and solutions presented here, readers are invited to join the ongoing conversation about how best to end the suffering and bring about a just resolution that honors the dignity and rights of all people involved.

The road to peace is undoubtedly long and difficult, but it is not beyond reach. Through careful analysis, empathy, and a commitment to justice, we can begin to chart a course that moves beyond the cycles of violence and toward a future where Israelis and Palestinians can coexist in mutual respect and security. This book is a contribution to that effort, offering hope and insight at a time when both are desperately needed.

3

Two-State Solution

The Two-State Solution has long been regarded as the most viable and equitable resolution to the Israel-Palestine conflict. It envisions the creation of an independent Palestinian state alongside Israel, where both nations coexist peacefully with recognized and secure borders. The concept gained prominence in the mid-20th century, especially after the 1948 Arab-Israeli War and the subsequent establishment of the State of Israel, which left a significant Palestinian population without a state of their own. The idea was further formalized by United Nations Resolution 181 in 1947, which proposed the partition of Palestine into separate Jewish and Arab states, with Jerusalem under international administration. While the resolution was accepted by the Jewish leadership, it was rejected by the Arab states and Palestinian leaders, leading to decades of conflict and failed negotiations.

The core idea of the Two-State Solution is to establish a Palestinian state in the West Bank and Gaza Strip, territories occupied by Israel since the 1967 Six-Day War. The proposed borders would largely follow the pre-1967 lines, known as the Green Line, with mutually agreed land swaps to accommodate large Israeli settlements that have been built in the West Bank over the past several decades. These settlements have been a major sticking point in negotiations, as they are considered illegal under international law, though Israel disputes this. The land swaps would allow Israel to retain some of these settlements in exchange for providing the Palestinians with equivalent land from within Israel's pre-1967 territory. The exact details of these swaps would need to be carefully negotiated to ensure both sides find the arrangement acceptable.

Jerusalem, a city of profound religious and historical significance to both Jews and Arabs, is another central issue in the Two-State Solution. The city was divided between Israel and Jordan from 1948 until 1967, when Israel captured East Jerusalem during the Six-Day War and later annexed it, a move not recognized by the international community. For a Two-State Solution to succeed, a compromise on Jerusalem's status is essential. One proposal is to divide the city, with West Jerusalem serving as the capital of Israel and East Jerusalem as the capital of Palestine. Another suggestion is to keep Jerusalem as a shared capital, with both states having administrative control over their respective parts of the city while ensuring open access to religious sites for all faiths. The complexity of Jerusalem's religious and cultural importance makes this a particularly challenging aspect of any peace agreement.

The issue of Palestinian refugees is also a significant challenge in the Two-State Solution. Over 700,000 Palestinians were displaced during the 1948 Arab-Israeli War, and their descendants now number in the millions. The right of return for these refugees has been a longstanding demand of the Palestinian leadership, but Israel has consistently opposed it, fearing that an influx of Palestinian refugees could threaten the Jewish character of the state. A potential compromise might involve offering refugees the option to return to the new Palestinian state, receive compensation, or resettle in third countries, with a limited number allowed to return to Israel under specific conditions. This approach aims to balance the rights and aspirations of the refugees with Israel's demographic concerns.

Security is another critical component of the Two-State Solution. Both Israel and Palestine would need robust security arrangements to prevent future conflicts and ensure the safety of their citizens. For Israel, this includes concerns about potential threats from militant groups within a future Palestinian state, particularly in Gaza, where Hamas remains in control. Possible security measures could include demilitarizing the Palestinian state, establishing an international peacekeeping force to monitor borders, and ensuring close cooperation between Israeli and Palestinian security forces. Additionally, international guarantees from major powers and regional actors could play a role in providing long-term security assurances.

While the Two-State Solution offers a clear framework for resolving the Israel-Palestine conflict, it faces significant obstacles. The expansion of Israeli settlements in the West Bank, political divisions within both Israeli and Palestinian leadership, and the broader regional dynamics, including the influence of neighboring Arab states and Iran, all complicate the path to peace. Moreover, public opinion on both sides has become increasingly skeptical of the feasibility of the Two-State Solution, with many Palestinians feeling that it does not adequately address their rights, and many Israelis doubting that a Palestinian state would be a peaceful neighbor. Despite these challenges, the Two-State Solution remains the cornerstone of international efforts to achieve peace in the region. It represents a compromise that, while difficult, could potentially satisfy the core aspirations of both peoples: security and sovereignty for Israelis, and statehood and dignity for Palestinians. The success of this solution ultimately depends on the willingness of both sides to make painful compromises and the active involvement of the international community in facilitating and supporting the peace process.

The success of the Two-State Solution hinges not only on the willingness of Israeli and Palestinian leaders to make concessions but also on the broader support of their respective populations and the international community. Public sentiment plays a crucial role in shaping the political landscape, and over the years, both Israeli and Palestinian societies have experienced shifts in attitudes toward peace and compromise. In Israel, the rise of right-wing politics and the expansion of settlements have fueled skepticism about the feasibility of a Palestinian state. Many Israelis fear that withdrawing from the West Bank could lead to increased security risks, similar to the situation in Gaza following Israel's disengagement in 2005. This fear is exacerbated by the ongoing rocket attacks from Gaza and the influence of militant groups like Hamas, which oppose Israel's existence and reject the Two-State Solution.

On the Palestinian side, years of occupation, settlement expansion, and failed negotiations have led to growing disillusionment with the peace process. Many Palestinians view the Two-State Solution as increasingly unrealistic, given the physical and political fragmentation of the West Bank and the isolation of Gaza. The split between the Palestinian Authority, which governs parts of the West Bank, and Hamas, which controls Gaza, further complicates the prospects for a unified Palestinian leadership capable of negotiating and implementing a peace agreement. Additionally, the younger generation of Palestinians, who have grown up during the years of the Oslo Accords and the subsequent disappointments, are often more radicalized and less inclined to accept compromises that do not fully address their aspirations for justice, statehood, and the right of return.

Despite these challenges, the Two-State Solution remains the most widely endorsed framework for resolving the conflict, particularly within the international community. The United Nations, the European Union, the United States, and many Arab states have consistently supported the idea of two states living side by side in peace. However, translating this broad international consensus into actionable steps on the ground has proven elusive. Various peace initiatives, such as the Camp David Summit in 2000, the Annapolis Conference in 2007, and more recently, the U.S.-led "Deal of the Century" proposed by the Trump administration, have all fallen short of achieving a lasting resolution. These failures underscore the complexity of the issues at hand and the deep-seated mistrust between the parties.

For the Two-State Solution to become a reality, several critical conditions must be met. First, there must be a genuine commitment from both Israeli and Palestinian leaders to engage in good-faith negotiations, backed by a willingness to make significant and, at times, painful compromises. This includes Israel's recognition of the need to halt settlement expansion and consider territorial concessions, and the Palestinian leadership's acceptance of a compromise on the right of return and the renunciation of violence. Second, the international community must play an active role in facilitating and supporting the peace process, including providing guarantees for security arrangements, economic aid, and political backing for any agreement reached. This could involve a more robust involvement from the United Nations, the European Union, and key regional players like Egypt, Jordan, and Saudi Arabia, who have a vested interest in a stable and peaceful Middle East.

Third, there needs to be a concerted effort to build trust and understanding between ordinary Israelis and Palestinians. This can be achieved through grassroots initiatives that promote dialogue, reconciliation, and cooperation in areas such as education, culture, and economics. People-to-people programs, joint economic ventures, and cultural exchanges can help break down the barriers of mistrust and humanize the "other" side, paving the way for a more conducive environment for peace. Additionally, addressing the humanitarian and economic needs of the Palestinian population, particularly in Gaza, is essential to creating the conditions for a sustainable peace. This includes lifting the blockade on Gaza, improving infrastructure and living conditions, and ensuring access to education, healthcare, and employment opportunities.

Finally, any viable Two-State Solution must be grounded in a realistic and enforceable framework that addresses the core issues of borders, Jerusalem, refugees, and security. This framework should be based on international law and supported by robust enforcement mechanisms to ensure compliance by both parties. The role of third-party mediators, possibly including an international peacekeeping force or monitoring mission, could be crucial in maintaining peace and resolving disputes that may arise during the implementation of the agreement.

The Two-State Solution represents a path forward that, while fraught with challenges, offers the best hope for a just and lasting resolution to the Israel-Palestine conflict. It seeks to balance the legitimate aspirations of both peoples—Israelis' need for security and recognition, and Palestinians' right to self-determination and statehood. The road to peace is long and difficult, requiring courage, vision, and perseverance from all involved. Yet, the alternative—a continued cycle of violence, occupation, and despair—is far more costly. The Two-State Solution is not just a political compromise; it is a moral imperative for a region that has known too much suffering and conflict. The future of Israel and Palestine, and indeed the broader Middle East, depends on the ability of their leaders and peoples to embrace this vision of peace and work tirelessly to make it a reality.

Two-State Solution's potential to bring about a lasting peace hinges on addressing several critical issues that have been at the heart of the conflict for decades. These issues include the determination of borders, the status of Jerusalem, the right of return for Palestinian refugees, and the security guarantees necessary to ensure the safety of both states. Each of these components is complex and requires careful negotiation, compromise, and international support to achieve a workable solution.

One of the most contentious aspects of the Two-State Solution is the determination of borders. The 1967 borders, also known as the Green Line, have often been cited as the basis for the borders of the two states. However, the reality on the ground has changed significantly since 1967, with Israel having established numerous settlements in the West Bank, home to hundreds of thousands of Israeli citizens. These settlements complicate the drawing of borders, as they are interspersed throughout what would otherwise be Palestinian territory. The concept of land swaps has been proposed as a way to address this issue. Under this arrangement, Israel would annex some of the larger settlement blocs that are close to the Green Line, and in return, Palestine would receive land from within Israel's pre-1967 borders. This approach aims to create a more contiguous and viable Palestinian state while allowing Israel to retain key areas of settlement. However, the specific details of these land swaps, including which areas would be exchanged and how they would impact local populations, remain a matter of intense debate.

Jerusalem presents another formidable challenge. The city holds profound religious and cultural significance for Jews, Muslims, and Christians alike, making its status one of the most sensitive issues in the conflict. Israel considers Jerusalem its "eternal and undivided capital," while Palestinians see East Jerusalem, which Israel captured in 1967 and later annexed, as the capital of their future state. Various proposals have been put forward to address the issue of Jerusalem in the context of a Two-State Solution. One option is to divide the city, with West Jerusalem serving as the capital of Israel and East Jerusalem as the capital of Palestine. Another proposal involves establishing a special international regime to govern the city, particularly the Old City, which contains key religious sites. This would ensure that the religious rights of all faiths are protected, and that the city remains accessible to people of all religions. A more recent suggestion is the idea of "shared sovereignty," where both Israel and Palestine would have administrative control over their respective parts of the city, while cooperating on issues of mutual concern. Each of these proposals seeks to balance the religious and national claims of both sides, but finding a solution that is acceptable to both Israelis and Palestinians remains a significant obstacle.

The right of return for Palestinian refugees is another core issue that must be addressed in any Two-State Solution. The Palestinian refugee problem dates back to the 1948 Arab-Israeli War, during which hundreds of thousands of Palestinians were displaced from their homes. Today, their descendants number in the millions, and the right of return is a deeply held demand among Palestinians. However, Israel has consistently opposed the mass return of Palestinian refugees, arguing that it would threaten the Jewish character of the state. A potential compromise might involve offering refugees several options: returning to the Palestinian state, receiving compensation for their lost property, or resettling in third countries with international assistance. This solution would aim to address the humanitarian needs of the refugees while ensuring that Israel's demographic concerns are taken into account. The issue of compensation, in particular, would require significant financial resources and international cooperation, but it could serve as a key component of a broader peace agreement.

Security is a paramount concern for both Israel and a future Palestinian state. Israel has legitimate concerns about the potential threats it could face from a neighboring Palestinian state, particularly given the presence of militant groups such as Hamas in Gaza, which continues to reject Israel's right to exist and has engaged in armed conflict with Israel on multiple occasions. For a Two-State Solution to be viable, robust security arrangements must be put in place to prevent the emergence of a security vacuum that could be exploited by extremists. One possible approach is the demilitarization of the Palestinian state, combined with international security guarantees. This could involve the deployment of international peacekeeping forces along the borders and in sensitive areas, such as Jerusalem, to monitor and enforce the terms of the peace agreement. Additionally, there would need to be close security cooperation between Israeli and Palestinian authorities to combat terrorism and maintain stability. The international community, particularly key stakeholders like the United States and the European Union, would play a critical role in providing the necessary security assurances and resources to support these efforts.

Despite the numerous challenges associated with the Two-State Solution, it remains the most widely endorsed framework for resolving the Israel-Palestine conflict. It is supported by a broad international consensus, including the United Nations, the European Union, and the Arab

League, which has repeatedly reaffirmed its commitment to the Arab Peace Initiative, a proposal that offers Israel full normalization of relations with the Arab world in exchange for its withdrawal from the occupied territories and the establishment of a Palestinian state. For the Two-State Solution to succeed, it will require not only bold leadership from both Israeli and Palestinian leaders but also sustained engagement and support from the international community. This includes diplomatic efforts to bring the parties back to the negotiating table, economic assistance to help build a viable Palestinian state, and a commitment to upholding international law and human rights.

The Two-State Solution offers a pathway to peace that, while difficult and fraught with challenges, has the potential to finally resolve the Israel-Palestine conflict in a way that respects the rights and aspirations of both peoples. It envisions a future where Israelis and Palestinians can live side by side in peace and security, each in their own state, with mutual recognition and respect. The road to achieving this vision will be long and difficult, requiring compromises and sacrifices on both sides, but it is a goal worth striving for. The alternative—continued conflict, occupation, and instability—is far too costly, not only for the people of Israel and Palestine but for the entire region and the world. The Two-State Solution is not just a diplomatic option; it is a moral imperative for all who seek a just and lasting peace in the Middle East.

The path toward realizing the Two-State Solution is undoubtedly challenging, but it is rooted in a vision of mutual coexistence and respect that could serve as a beacon of hope in an otherwise turbulent region. To move from concept to reality, several key steps must be undertaken, each fraught with its own set of difficulties but also rich with the potential for transformative change.

First and foremost, the political will on both sides must be galvanized to re-engage in serious negotiations. For years, peace talks have been marred by mutual distrust, political divisions, and the influence of hardline factions within both Israeli and Palestinian societies. For the Two-State Solution to succeed, both Israeli and Palestinian leaders must be prepared to make bold decisions that may be unpopular with segments of their constituencies. This requires not only strong leadership but also a clear and unwavering commitment to peace. On the Israeli side, this might mean halting the expansion of settlements and acknowledging the necessity of territorial compromise. On the Palestinian side, it could involve taking decisive steps to unify the political landscape, particularly the division between Fatah and Hamas, and to commit unequivocally to non-violence as the path to achieving national aspirations.

In parallel, the international community must step up its efforts to facilitate and support the peace process. This involves more than just diplomatic pressure; it requires a coordinated and sustained effort to address the economic, social, and security challenges that both Israelis and Palestinians face. For instance, the economic disparities between Israel and the Palestinian territories are vast, and addressing these disparities is crucial for the viability of a future Palestinian state. International aid, investment in infrastructure, and the promotion of economic cooperation between Israel and Palestine are essential components of building a stable and prosperous region. The European Union, the United States, and Arab states with vested interests in regional stability should lead in providing the necessary resources and incentives for both sides to remain committed to the peace process.

Moreover, the role of civil society cannot be understated in this endeavor. Grassroots movements, NGOs, and local leaders on both sides have the potential to build bridges where official diplomacy has failed. Initiatives that bring together Israelis and Palestinians in dialogue, joint economic projects, and cultural exchanges can help to humanize the "other" and reduce the pervasive mistrust that fuels the conflict. Education also plays a critical role in this context; promoting narratives that emphasize peace, coexistence, and mutual understanding in schools can help to foster a new generation that is more inclined toward reconciliation than conflict. These efforts, while small in scale compared to the broader geopolitical dynamics, are vital in laying the groundwork for a peace that is not just imposed from above but rooted in the everyday experiences and aspirations of ordinary people.

The legal and institutional frameworks necessary to support the Two-State Solution also require careful consideration. The creation of a Palestinian state will involve establishing institutions that can govern effectively and democratically, ensuring the rule of law, and protecting the rights of all citizens. This includes building a robust legal system, developing economic policies that promote growth and reduce poverty, and ensuring that the security forces are professional and accountable. For Israel, it will be important to ensure that any withdrawal from the West Bank is managed in a way that does not compromise its security, which might involve international guarantees or phased implementation of agreements to build confidence. The role of international organizations, such as the United Nations, in monitoring compliance with peace agreements and providing technical assistance in state-building, will be critical in this regard.

The regional and global context in which the Two-State Solution is pursued will have a significant impact on its prospects for success. The Middle East is a region marked by volatility, with conflicts in Syria, Lebanon, and Yemen, as well as the broader rivalry between Iran and Saudi Arabia, influencing the dynamics of the Israel-Palestine conflict. A comprehensive approach to peace in the region would benefit from addressing these broader conflicts and engaging regional powers in a constructive dialogue about the future of the Middle East. The normalization agreements between Israel and several Arab states, such as the United Arab Emirates and Bahrain, under the Abraham Accords, have shifted the regional landscape and could provide a foundation for broader regional cooperation, including on the Israel-Palestine issue. However, these agreements should not be seen as a substitute for resolving the Palestinian question but rather as an opportunity to build a broader coalition in support of the Two-State Solution.

While the Two-State Solution is not without its challenges, it remains the most realistic and morally compelling framework for resolving the Israel-Palestine conflict. It offers a path forward that acknowledges the legitimate rights and aspirations of both peoples while providing a basis for peace, security, and cooperation in a region that has known too much conflict and suffering. The journey to achieve this solution will require courage, compromise, and sustained effort from all parties involved—Israelis, Palestinians, and the international community alike. But the prize—lasting peace and the chance for future generations to live in harmony—is one that makes the struggle worthwhile. In the end, the success of the Two-State Solution will depend on our collective ability to imagine a different future, one where the history of conflict gives way to a new era of coexistence and mutual respect.

As the world looks toward the future, the urgency of resolving the Israel-Palestine conflict grows ever more apparent. The Two-State Solution, though fraught with challenges, offers a vision of peace that honors the rights and dignity of both Israelis and Palestinians. However, the road to realizing this vision is complex, requiring a multi-faceted approach that addresses the political, social, economic, and security dimensions of the conflict.

One of the most critical elements in advancing the Two-State Solution is fostering a culture of peace and mutual recognition. Over the decades, the conflict has fostered deep-seated animosities and mistrust between the two peoples. Overcoming these psychological barriers is as important as resolving the tangible issues of borders, security, and governance. For true peace to take root, both Israelis and Palestinians must come to see each other not as enemies but as neighbors with legitimate rights and aspirations. This shift in perception can be facilitated through dialogue initiatives, peace education programs, and public diplomacy efforts that emphasize common ground and shared humanity.

Additionally, the role of the international community remains indispensable in mediating and supporting the peace process. While the United States has traditionally played a leading role in Israeli-Palestinian negotiations, the involvement of other key actors—such as the European Union, Russia, and regional powers like Egypt and Jordan—can provide a more balanced and inclusive approach. These actors can offer fresh perspectives, additional resources, and critical diplomatic backing to ensure that any agreement reached is sustainable and enjoys broad international legitimacy. Moreover, international organizations like the United Nations can contribute by providing frameworks for negotiations, monitoring compliance, and assisting with post-agreement implementation.

Economic development is another cornerstone of the Two-State Solution. For a Palestinian state to be viable and stable, it must have a strong economic foundation that can provide for the needs of its people. This includes developing infrastructure, fostering entrepreneurship, and integrating the Palestinian economy into regional and global markets. International investment, coupled with policies that promote trade and economic cooperation between Israel and Palestine, can help to create jobs, reduce poverty, and build the economic interdependence that is often a key ingredient in sustaining peace. Israel, with its advanced economy, stands to benefit from a stable and prosperous Palestinian neighbor, which could open up new opportunities for trade, tourism, and regional cooperation.

Security concerns are at the heart of the Israeli-Palestinian conflict, and any resolution must address these concerns comprehensively. For Israel, ensuring that a future Palestinian state does not become a base for terrorism or military threats is paramount. For Palestinians, achieving security means freedom from occupation and the establishment of sovereignty over their own land. A balanced approach to security would involve robust international guarantees, such as the deployment of peacekeeping forces or international monitors, to oversee the implementation of the peace agreement and prevent violence. Additionally, joint Israeli-Palestinian security arrangements, perhaps with the support of international partners, could help to build trust and cooperation in the security domain.

The status of Jerusalem remains one of the most sensitive and symbolic issues in the conflict. As the city holds deep religious significance for Jews, Muslims, and Christians, any agreement must respect the rights and access of all faiths. While various models have been proposed—ranging from shared sovereignty to international administration—the solution must ultimately reflect the aspirations of both Israelis and Palestinians while preserving the city's unique character as a center of religious and cultural heritage. Creative solutions, such as a unified but administratively divided Jerusalem, or a city with dual capitals, could help to bridge the gap between the competing claims.

In addressing the Palestinian refugee issue, it is crucial to find a solution that balances the refugees' right to return with the realities of the present-day situation. Compensation, resettlement options, and limited return to the new Palestinian state could be part of a comprehensive agreement that honors the refugees' historical experiences while ensuring the stability and identity of both states. International support, both financial and logistical, will be necessary to implement any agreement on this issue, which remains one of the most emotionally charged aspects of the conflict.

The success of the Two-State Solution will depend on the willingness of both sides to engage in genuine, sustained negotiations and to make the difficult compromises necessary for peace. It will require leadership that is not only politically astute but also morally courageous—leaders who are willing to look beyond short-term political gains to the long-term benefits of peace for their people. This leadership must be supported by their societies, which means that public opinion on both sides must be prepared for the sacrifices and changes that a peace agreement will entail.

The international community, too, has a role to play in creating the conditions for successful negotiations. This includes not only diplomatic efforts but also providing the necessary economic and security support to ensure that a peace agreement can be implemented effectively. The lessons of past negotiations must be learned and applied, recognizing that the process of peace-building is as important as the final agreement itself.

As we look to the future, it is clear that the Two-State Solution remains the most viable path to achieving a just and lasting peace between Israelis and Palestinians. It offers a framework that respects the national aspirations of both peoples, provides for their security, and lays the groundwork for a peaceful and prosperous future. While the road ahead is challenging, it is also full of opportunities for those willing to take the necessary steps toward peace. The time to act is now, before the window for a Two-State Solution closes, and the opportunity for peace is lost to the forces of extremism and despair. This book aims to contribute to that effort, by exploring the complexities of the conflict and the potential solutions, and by encouraging all who read it to think critically, act justly, and work tirelessly for peace.

4

One-State Solution

The One-State Solution proposes an alternative approach to resolving the Israel-Palestine conflict by establishing a single, binational state in which both Israelis and Palestinians live together with equal rights. This idea challenges the notion of dividing the land into two separate states and instead envisions a unified state where people of all ethnicities and religions coexist under a single government. The One-State Solution addresses several core issues of the conflict by focusing on equality, shared governance, and cultural autonomy.

At the heart of the One-State Solution is the principle of equal citizenship. In this envisioned state, every resident, whether Israeli or Palestinian, would be granted equal rights and citizenship, regardless of their ethnicity, religion, or national identity. This would mean that all citizens would have the same legal status, the right to vote, access to public services, and protection under the law. The idea is to move beyond the current system, where rights and privileges are often determined by one's ethnic or religious background, and instead create a society based on universal human rights and equality. For many proponents of this solution, equal citizenship is seen as the most just and ethical way to resolve the conflict, as it seeks to eliminate the systemic inequalities and discrimination that have fueled tensions for decades.

Shared governance is another key component of the One-State Solution. The governance of this binational state would require a system that fairly represents both Israeli and Palestinian communities. This could take the form of a power-sharing arrangement, where political power is distributed between the two groups to ensure that neither dominates the other. Such a system might include a bicameral legislature, with one house representing the population proportionally and another designed to protect the interests of both communities equally. Alternatively, a rotating presidency or a co-presidency could be implemented, where leadership is shared between representatives from both groups. The goal of shared governance is to create a political structure that is inclusive and responsive to the needs of all citizens, thereby fostering a sense of ownership and participation across the entire population.

Cultural autonomy is also central to the One-State Solution. Given the deep cultural and religious differences between Israelis and Palestinians, the solution would allow for a degree of cultural and religious autonomy within the framework of a single state. This could involve recognizing and preserving the distinct identities, languages, and traditions of both communities, while promoting mutual respect and understanding. For instance, different regions within the state could have the authority to govern their own educational systems, cultural institutions, and religious practices, allowing each community to maintain its unique heritage while coexisting within a broader national identity. Cultural autonomy seeks to balance the need for unity with the recognition of diversity, ensuring that the new state does not erase the distinct identities of its citizens but instead celebrates and protects them.

The One-State Solution is appealing to some because it promises to resolve many of the issues that have stymied other peace efforts, such as the disputes over borders, settlements, and the status of Jerusalem. By eliminating the need to divide the land, it sidesteps the contentious issue of where to draw the borders between Israel and a future Palestinian state. Additionally, it addresses the problem of Israeli settlements in the West Bank by integrating them into the new state rather than requiring their dismantlement or annexation. Jerusalem, a city of profound significance to both Israelis and Palestinians, would also remain undivided, serving as the capital for all citizens.

However, the One-State Solution is not without its challenges and critics. One of the main concerns is the feasibility of creating a state that truly provides equal rights and representation for both communities. Given the historical animosities and deep-seated mistrust between

Israelis and Palestinians, there is a fear that one group might dominate the other, leading to further conflict and instability. Critics argue that the cultural, religious, and national differences between the two groups are too great to be reconciled within a single state, and that attempting to do so could result in a fragile and volatile political system. Moreover, the One-State Solution raises questions about the future identity of the state—whether it would remain a Jewish state, as Israel is today, or evolve into a secular, multicultural state that reflects the diversity of its population.

Another significant challenge is the lack of political support for the One-State Solution among both Israeli and Palestinian leadership. For many Israelis, the idea of a single state with a Palestinian majority is seen as a threat to the Jewish character of Israel. For Palestinians, the concern is that a single state might not truly deliver equality but instead perpetuate the existing power imbalances. These concerns are reflected in public opinion as well, where support for the One-State Solution remains relatively low compared to other proposed solutions.

Despite these challenges, the One-State Solution continues to be discussed as a potential pathway to peace, particularly as the viability of the Two-State Solution becomes increasingly uncertain. Proponents argue that, given the realities on the ground—such as the deep integration of Israeli settlements in the West Bank and the demographic trends that suggest a future Palestinian majority in the land between the Jordan River and the Mediterranean Sea—the One-State Solution might be the only realistic option left. They also point to examples of successful binational states around the world as evidence that such a solution can work, provided there is a genuine commitment to equality, justice, and democracy.

The One-State Solution presents a bold and controversial alternative to the longstanding Israel-Palestine conflict. It challenges traditional notions of statehood and sovereignty by proposing a shared future for two peoples who have long been at odds. While the road to achieving such a solution would undoubtedly be difficult, with significant obstacles to overcome, it also holds the promise of creating a state where Israelis and Palestinians can live together in peace, equality, and mutual respect. Whether this solution can be realized will depend on the willingness of both sides to re-imagine their future and embrace a vision of shared citizenship and governance that transcends the divisions of the past.

The potential success of the One-State Solution largely depends on several critical factors that would need to be addressed to ensure that the unified state does not merely replicate existing inequalities or create new ones. The first and perhaps most fundamental challenge is creating a robust framework for equal citizenship. In practice, this would require significant legal and institutional reforms to guarantee that all residents—regardless of their ethnic or religious background—have the same rights and opportunities. This includes not only the right to vote and run for office but also equal access to education, healthcare, housing, and employment. The legal system would need to be designed to protect against discrimination, and mechanisms for enforcing these rights would need to be strong and transparent.

One of the key concerns in implementing equal citizenship in a unified state is the question of demographic balance. Currently, Jewish Israelis form a majority within Israel's recognized borders, while Palestinians form the majority in the West Bank and Gaza. If the two populations were combined into a single state, the demographic balance would shift significantly, with potentially far-reaching political and social implications. Some Israelis fear that this shift could lead to a loss of political power and cultural identity, particularly if Palestinians were to become the majority. On the other hand, Palestinians might worry that despite being granted equal citizenship on paper, they could still face systemic discrimination and marginalization in practice.

To address these concerns, the unified state would need to establish clear and fair rules for shared governance. This might involve creating a power-sharing system that ensures both communities are represented in key political institutions. For example, a bicameral legislature could be established, with one chamber representing the population proportionally and the other ensuring equal representation for both communities, regardless of their population size. Additionally, a rotating presidency or co-presidency could be considered, allowing leaders from both communities to share executive power. The goal of such arrangements would be to prevent any single group from dominating the political system and to foster a sense of shared ownership and responsibility for the state's future.

Cultural autonomy would also play a crucial role in the One-State Solution. Given the deep cultural and religious differences between Israelis and Palestinians, the state would need to allow for a degree of autonomy in cultural and religious matters. This could include allowing different regions or communities to govern their own educational systems, religious institutions, and cultural practices. Such autonomy would help preserve the distinct identities of both communities while promoting mutual respect and understanding. It would also be essential to create spaces for dialogue and cooperation between the communities, fostering a sense of unity within diversity.

The One-State Solution could potentially resolve some of the most intractable issues in the Israel-Palestine conflict, such as the disputes over borders and the status of Jerusalem. By unifying the land under a single state, the need to draw contentious borders would be eliminated, and Jerusalem could remain an undivided city, serving as a capital for all citizens. This approach would also address the issue of Israeli settlements in the West Bank, as they would be integrated into the new state rather than requiring dismantlement or annexation.

However, the One-State Solution faces significant challenges and opposition. Many Israelis view the idea of a single state with a Palestinian majority as a threat to the Jewish character of Israel. For Palestinians, there is a concern that the promise of equal citizenship might not be fully realized, and that the power dynamics of the current situation could persist in the new state. Additionally, there is little political support for the One-State Solution among the leadership of both communities, making it difficult to see how such a solution could be implemented in the near term.

Despite these obstacles, some advocates argue that the One-State Solution may be the only viable option left, given the realities on the ground. The continued expansion of Israeli settlements in the West Bank, the integration of the economies and infrastructure of the two populations, and the demographic trends suggest that the possibility of separating the two communities into distinct states is becoming increasingly remote. For these advocates, the focus should now be on creating a state that can accommodate the needs and aspirations of both peoples, rather than trying to divide them further.

The One-State Solution represents a bold and challenging alternative to the traditional two-state approach. It envisions a future where Israelis and Palestinians live together as equal citizens in a single, democratic state. While this solution offers the potential to address many of the issues that have stymied other peace efforts, it also requires a profound rethinking of national identities, political structures, and the nature of the state itself. Whether or not the One-State Solution can be realized will depend on the willingness of both communities to embrace a new vision of their future—one that is rooted in equality, justice, and shared sovereignty. The path to achieving this vision is fraught with difficulties, but for some, it represents the most promising hope for a lasting and just peace in the region.

The One-State Solution, while offering a vision of equality and co-existence, also raises significant concerns about its feasibility and the potential risks involved. One of the primary challenges is how to ensure that the rights and identities of both Israelis and Palestinians are genuinely respected and protected in a single state. Given the historical context of conflict and deep-seated mistrust, building a shared national identity that encompasses both groups could be extremely difficult.

For many Israelis, the idea of a single state is seen as a threat to the Jewish character of Israel. Israel was founded as a Jewish state, a homeland for Jews after centuries of persecution and the horrors of the Holocaust. The concern is that in a binational state where Palestinians might eventually become the majority, the Jewish character of the state could be diluted or lost altogether. This fear is not just about demographics but also about cultural, religious, and political influence. Israelis might worry that their traditions, language, and way of life could be overshadowed in a state where they are no longer the majority.

On the Palestinian side, there is a deep concern that a one-state framework might not truly deliver the equality it promises. Palestinians could fear that the existing power structures, which currently favor Israeli interests, would continue to do so, even in a unified state. They might worry that despite formal equality, the realities of political and economic power would still leave them marginalized. There is also a fear that the Palestinian national identity could be eroded in a state that is not explicitly Palestinian, as it would be in an independent Palestinian state.

To address these concerns, advocates of the One-State Solution argue that the state must be founded on principles of genuine equality and inclusiveness. This means not only equal legal rights but also ensuring that both communities have meaningful representation and influence in the political, cultural, and economic life of the state. This could involve creating a constitution that guarantees the protection of minority rights and provides mechanisms for power-sharing at all levels of government.

Another major challenge is the integration of the two populations. After decades of separation, with Palestinians largely confined to the West Bank, Gaza, and East Jerusalem, and Israelis primarily living within Israel's pre-1967 borders, there is little interaction between the two communities. This lack of contact has fostered stereotypes, prejudices, and a lack of understanding. A successful One-State Solution would require significant efforts to bridge these divides, fostering a sense of common citizenship and shared future. This could involve large-scale educational reforms, media campaigns promoting tolerance and understanding, and initiatives that bring Israelis and Palestinians together in shared projects and community-building efforts.

Economic integration would also be a crucial factor in the success of a unified state. Currently, there are vast disparities between the Israeli and Palestinian economies, with Israelis enjoying a much higher standard of living. These economic inequalities would need to be addressed to prevent the perpetuation of existing power imbalances. This might involve significant investment in Palestinian infrastructure, education, and healthcare, as well as policies aimed at creating economic opportunities for all citizens, regardless of their background. The international community could play a key role in supporting these efforts, providing financial assistance and expertise to help build a more balanced and integrated economy.

Security concerns would remain a critical issue in any discussion of a One-State Solution. Given the history of violence and mistrust, both communities would need strong assurances that their security would be protected in a unified state. This might involve creating joint security forces composed of both Israelis and Palestinians, along with international oversight to ensure that these forces operate fairly and impartially. It would also be important to develop a comprehensive approach to countering extremism on both sides, promoting a narrative of peace and coexistence rather than conflict.

In the broader regional and international context, the One-State Solution would require a shift in how the conflict is approached by global powers. The international community, which has long supported the Two-State Solution, would need to consider how to support a transition to a single state if that became the chosen path. This could involve diplomatic efforts to ensure that both Israelis and Palestinians feel secure and respected in the new state, as well as economic and technical support for the challenges of integration and state-building.

Despite the significant challenges, some believe that the One-State Solution offers the best hope for a sustainable and just peace. The argument is that the realities on the ground—such as the deep integration of Israeli settlements in the West Bank and the growing interdependence of the two economies—make the creation of two separate states increasingly unfeasible. Proponents of the One-State Solution argue that rather than trying to divide the land and people further, it would be more productive to focus on creating a state that can accommodate the needs and aspirations of both peoples.

In conclusion, the One-State Solution is a complex and controversial proposal that challenges the traditional approaches to resolving the Israel-Palestine conflict. It envisions a future where Israelis and Palestinians live together in a single, democratic state with equal rights for all. While this vision offers the potential for a more inclusive and just society, it also raises significant concerns about identity, governance, and security. Whether the One-State Solution can be realized will depend on the willingness of both communities to engage in a process of reconciliation and to reimagine their future in a way that transcends the divisions of the past. It is a path that requires courage, creativity, and a deep commitment to the principles of equality and justice.

5

Confederation Model

The Confederation Model offers a middle ground between the Two-State and One-State Solutions by proposing two sovereign states, Israel and Palestine, that operate within a framework of close cooperation, shared resources, and open borders. This model aims to address the aspirations of both Israelis and Palestinians for national self-determination while recognizing the practical realities of their intertwined geographies, economies, and security concerns. Unlike a complete separation of the two states or a fully integrated single state, the Confederation Model allows for both autonomy and interdependence, creating a unique approach to conflict resolution that emphasizes collaboration over division.

The core idea of the Confederation Model is to establish Israel and Palestine as two distinct and independent states, each with its own government, legal system, and national identity. However, rather than existing in isolation from one another, these states would engage in extensive cooperation through a network of shared institutions and policies. This cooperative framework would allow both states to manage shared resources, coordinate on security, and facilitate the movement of people and goods across borders, thereby enhancing the stability and prosperity of the entire region.

One of the key components of the Confederation Model is the creation of shared institutions. These institutions would be jointly managed by both Israel and Palestine and would oversee critical areas of mutual concern, such as water resources, infrastructure, environmental protection, and economic development. For example, water is a vital resource in the region, and both Israelis and Palestinians rely on shared water sources such as the Jordan River and various underground aquifers. By establishing a joint water management authority, the two states could work together to ensure the fair and sustainable use of water resources, reducing the potential for conflict over this essential commodity.

In addition to resource management, shared institutions could also play a role in economic cooperation. The economies of Israel and Palestine are already deeply interconnected, with many Palestinians working in Israel or in Israeli-owned businesses in the West Bank. Under the Confederation Model, the two states could create joint economic zones or industrial parks that benefit from the strengths of both economies. Such zones could attract international investment, create jobs, and boost economic growth for both Israelis and Palestinians. Moreover, by aligning economic policies and regulations, the two states could reduce barriers to trade and investment, leading to greater economic integration and mutual prosperity.

Open borders are another fundamental aspect of the Confederation Model. Unlike the strict separation envisioned in the traditional Two-State Solution, the Confederation Model allows for the free movement of people and goods between Israel and Palestine. This open border policy would enable Palestinians to travel freely to Israel for work, education, or family visits, and vice versa. It would also facilitate trade and commerce, allowing businesses in both states to access larger markets and reduce the costs associated with border controls and tariffs. An open border system would require careful management and security coordination to prevent illegal activities and ensure that the movement of people and goods is safe and orderly.

The concept of open borders also ties into the broader goal of social integration and cooperation between the two populations. By allowing people to move freely across the borders, the Confederation Model could help break down barriers and build trust between Israelis and Palestinians. Over time, increased interaction and collaboration could foster a sense of shared destiny and reduce the animosities that have fueled the conflict for so long. However, achieving this level of openness would require significant efforts to ensure that both populations feel secure and that their rights are respected.

Security cooperation is perhaps the most crucial component of the Confederation Model. Given the history of violence and mistrust between Israelis and Palestinians, any successful confederation would need to have robust security arrangements in place. These arrangements would involve close coordination between the security forces of both states, as well as joint efforts to combat terrorism, prevent cross-border attacks, and maintain public order. A shared security council or joint command structure could be established to oversee these efforts, ensuring that both sides have a say in security decisions and that responses to threats are coordinated and effective.

In addition to bilateral security cooperation, the Confederation Model could also benefit from international support. The presence of international peacekeepers or observers could help to build confidence in the security arrangements and provide an impartial mechanism for resolving disputes. International guarantees and support for the security framework would be essential in maintaining peace and stability, especially during the early stages of the confederation.

The Confederation Model also addresses the issue of Jerusalem, a city of profound importance to both Israelis and Palestinians. In this model, Jerusalem could serve as the capital of both states, with shared governance over the city. The confederation could establish a special administrative zone for Jerusalem, managed by a joint council representing both Israel and Palestine, along with international representatives. This council would oversee key aspects of the city's governance, including security, infrastructure, and the protection of religious sites. Such an arrangement would allow both Israelis and Palestinians to claim Jerusalem as their capital while ensuring that the city's unique religious and cultural significance is respected and preserved.

Despite its potential advantages, the Confederation Model is not without challenges. One of the main concerns is the level of trust required for such a system to function effectively. Given the deep-seated mistrust between Israelis and Palestinians, building the necessary trust and cooperation could be a long and difficult process. Both sides would need to be committed to the principles of the confederation and willing to work together in good faith. Another challenge is the complexity of managing shared institutions and coordinating policies across two sovereign states. This would require a high degree of political will and the development of new governance structures that are capable of managing the intricate relationships between the two states.

Moreover, the Confederation Model would likely face opposition from those who prefer a more traditional Two-State Solution or those who advocate for a single state. Some Israelis might fear that a confederation could undermine Israel's sovereignty or security, while some Palestinians might be concerned that it could limit their independence and self-determination. Overcoming these objections would require clear communication of the benefits of the confederation and assurances that both states' core interests would be protected.

The Confederation Model offers a novel approach to resolving the Israel-Palestine conflict, one that balances the desire for national self-determination with the practical need for cooperation and coexistence. By establishing two sovereign states within a framework of shared institutions, open borders, and coordinated security, the Confederation Model seeks to create a peaceful and prosperous future for both Israelis and Palestinians. While the challenges are significant, the potential rewards—a stable, secure, and cooperative region—make this model an option worth serious consideration. Whether it can be realized will depend on the willingness of both sides to embrace a vision of partnership and interdependence, and to work together to build a future that bene-fits all.

The Confederation Model, while presenting a compelling vision of shared sovereignty and cooperation, also requires addressing several crit-ical practicalities to ensure its success. For the model to work effectively, both Israel and Palestine would need to agree on the nature and scope of their shared institutions, the management of their open borders, and the specifics of their security cooperation. These elements are not just theoretical constructs but would require detailed planning, negoti-ations, and, most importantly, mutual trust.

One of the most significant challenges in implementing the Confed-eration Model is defining the scope and authority of shared institutions. These institutions would need to be designed in such a way that they respect the sovereignty of both states while effectively managing areas of common interest. The success of these institutions would hinge on their ability to operate impartially and transparently, ensuring that nei-ther state feels disadvantaged. For instance, a joint water management authority would need to allocate water resources equitably, considering the needs of both populations, agricultural demands, and environmen-tal sustainability. Similarly, shared economic zones would need to be managed in a way that benefits both economies, fostering growth and reducing economic disparities.

Another critical aspect of the Confederation Model is the establish-ment of open borders. The idea of open borders is appealing as it allows for the free movement of people and goods, which can promote eco-nomic growth and social integration. However, the implementation of such a policy would require careful planning to avoid potential pitfalls, such as the risk of uncontrolled migration or the smuggling of goods. Both states would need to agree on comprehensive border management policies, including the establishment of customs and immigration controls that facilitate movement while maintaining security. The success of open borders would also depend on the economic policies of both states being harmonized to some extent, to prevent significant imbalances that could lead to one state benefiting disproportionately from the arrangement.

Security cooperation is arguably the most complex and sensitive component of the Confederation Model. The history of conflict between Israelis and Palestinians has left deep scars, and both sides have legitimate security concerns that must be addressed. In a confederation, security cooperation would need to be closely coordinated, with both states working together to prevent violence and ensure stability. This could involve the establishment of a joint security council, which would oversee all aspects of security coordination, from intelligence sharing to joint patrols in sensitive areas. The success of this security cooperation would depend on building trust between the two security forces, which could be achieved through joint training programs, regular communication, and the development of shared standard operating procedures.

The role of international support in the Confederation Model cannot be understated. The international community could play a crucial role in facilitating the establishment of the confederation by providing financial support, technical expertise, and diplomatic backing. International peacekeeping forces or observers could also be deployed to help monitor the implementation of the confederation agreements and to provide a neutral party to mediate any disputes that arise. Additionally, international guarantees of the confederation's security arrangements could help reassure both states that their sovereignty and security will be respected.

The issue of Jerusalem remains a central challenge in any proposed solution to the Israel-Palestine conflict, including the Confederation Model. As the city holds deep religious and historical significance for both Israelis and Palestinians, finding a way to share and govern Jerusalem is critical. The Confederation Model could offer a creative solution by establishing Jerusalem as a shared capital, with a special administrative zone managed by a joint council. This council could include representatives from both states, as well as international observers, to oversee the city's governance, security, and preservation of religious sites. By ensuring that Jerusalem remains accessible to people of all faiths and that its cultural heritage is protected, the confederation could help to defuse one of the most contentious issues in the conflict.

The economic dimension of the Confederation Model also offers opportunities for cooperation and mutual benefit. By creating shared economic zones and aligning certain economic policies, Israel and Palestine could enhance their economic interdependence, which in turn could foster greater political stability. For example, joint infrastructure projects, such as transportation networks, energy grids, and telecommunications systems, could be developed to serve both states, reducing costs and improving efficiency. Additionally, the confederation could negotiate trade agreements with other countries and regional blocs, further integrating the Israeli and Palestinian economies into the global market.

However, the Confederation Model is not without its critics and potential obstacles. Some Israelis might fear that a confederation could lead to a gradual erosion of Israel's sovereignty, particularly if the shared institutions gain more power over time. There is also a concern that open borders could lead to security risks, especially if not managed effectively. On the Palestinian side, there might be concerns that the confederation could limit their sovereignty and that they might not achieve the level of independence they aspire to. These concerns would need to be addressed through careful negotiations, clear legal frameworks, and assurances that both states retain their full sovereignty within the confederation.

Another challenge is the political will to implement the Confederation Model. Both Israeli and Palestinian leaders would need to commit to the vision of a confederation and be willing to make the necessary compromises. This could be difficult, given the entrenched positions on both sides and the influence of hardline factions that oppose any form of cooperation. Building broad-based support for the confederation among the populations of both states would be essential, which could involve public awareness campaigns, educational programs, and dialogues aimed at explaining the benefits of the model and addressing concerns.

The Confederation Model presents a novel and potentially viable approach to resolving the Israel-Palestine conflict. By combining the advantages of sovereignty with the benefits of close cooperation, the model seeks to create a framework in which both Israelis and Palestinians can achieve their national aspirations while living side by side in peace. The success of the Confederation Model would depend on the willingness of both sides to embrace cooperation and mutual respect, as well as the support of the international community in facilitating the process. While the challenges are significant, the potential for a stable, prosperous, and peaceful future for both Israelis and Palestinians makes the Confederation Model an option worth serious consideration.

The Confederation Model, while offering a potentially transformative approach to the Israel-Palestine conflict, would also necessitate profound shifts in both the political landscapes and the societal attitudes of the two nations involved. The model's emphasis on shared institutions, open borders, and security cooperation would require not just political agreements, but also a deep commitment to building mutual trust and understanding among Israelis and Palestinians.

A successful confederation would need to be underpinned by a strong and inclusive legal framework. This framework would have to clearly delineate the powers and responsibilities of the shared institutions, as well as those of the individual states. It would need to establish mechanisms for resolving disputes between the two states and ensuring that both parties adhere to the agreements they have made. For example, a constitutional court or a similar legal body could be created to arbitrate any conflicts that arise between Israel and Palestine, ensuring that decisions are based on law rather than political considerations. This would help to build confidence in the confederation's stability and fairness.

Education and cultural exchange would play crucial roles in supporting the Confederation Model. Overcoming decades of mistrust and hostility would not be easy, but by fostering greater understanding and respect between the two peoples, the confederation could help to lay the groundwork for lasting peace. Educational initiatives could include joint schools, where Israeli and Palestinian children learn together about each other's histories, cultures, and perspectives. Cultural exchange programs, including art, music, and sports, could also be encouraged to build bridges between the two communities. These efforts would help to humanize the "other" and break down the stereotypes that have been perpetuated by years of conflict.

Economic cooperation, as mentioned earlier, would be another cornerstone of the Confederation Model. By creating an integrated economic space, the confederation could unlock new opportunities for growth and development that benefit both Israelis and Palestinians. This could involve coordinated economic policies, joint infrastructure projects, and the creation of a common market that allows for the free flow of goods, services, and labor. Such economic interdependence would not only improve living standards but also create strong incentives for maintaining peace and stability. Additionally, the confederation could attract international investment by presenting a more stable and cooperative environment, which could further boost economic development in the region.

The role of civil society in supporting the Confederation Model should not be underestimated. NGOs, community groups, and grassroots organizations could play a key role in promoting the confederation, educating the public about its benefits, and holding the governments of both states accountable for their commitments. These organizations could also help to facilitate dialogue and reconciliation between Israelis and Palestinians, addressing grievances and building a shared vision for the future. Moreover, civil society could serve as a bridge between the official negotiations and the broader public, ensuring that the voices of ordinary people are heard in the process of building the confederation.

International diplomacy would also be critical in supporting the Confederation Model. The international community, particularly key stakeholders like the United States, the European Union, and Arab states, would need to provide diplomatic backing for the confederation and encourage both Israel and Palestine to commit to the necessary compromises. This could involve diplomatic pressure, incentives, and guarantees to ensure that the confederation remains on track. Additionally, international organizations such as the United Nations could play a role in monitoring the implementation of the confederation agreements and providing technical assistance where needed.

The success of the Confederation Model would also depend on managing the expectations and concerns of both populations. Israelis would need to be reassured that their security and sovereignty would not be compromised, and that the confederation would not lead to the dilution of their national identity. Palestinians, on the other hand, would need guarantees that the confederation would not limit their independence or perpetuate existing inequalities. Addressing these concerns would require transparent communication, inclusive decision-making processes, and a commitment to upholding the principles of equality and justice for all citizens.

In the end, the Confederation Model offers a vision of a future where Israelis and Palestinians can live side by side, each with their own state but working together in a framework of mutual respect and cooperation. While this model presents significant challenges, it also holds the promise of a more stable, prosperous, and peaceful region. The success of this model would depend on the willingness of both sides to move beyond the zero-sum mentality that has dominated the conflict for so long, and to embrace a new paradigm of partnership and interdependence.

As the world continues to grapple with the complexities of the Israel-Palestine conflict, the Confederation Model provides a fresh and innovative approach that merits serious consideration. It challenges the traditional dichotomy between separation and integration, offering a middle path that seeks to combine the best of both worlds. Whether or not this model can be realized will depend on the courage and vision of leaders on both sides, as well as the support of the international community. But if it can be achieved, the Confederation Model could serve as a powerful example of how even the most intractable conflicts can be resolved through cooperation, creativity, and a shared commitment to peace.

The Confederation Model, by proposing a structure of cooperation between two sovereign states, represents a departure from the traditional approaches that have dominated peace efforts in the Israel-Palestine conflict. This model recognizes the interconnectedness of the two peoples and the practical realities that make a complete separation difficult, if not impossible. By fostering a relationship based on mutual interests, shared resources, and coordinated security, the Confederation Model aims to create a durable peace that is grounded in the everyday lives of Israelis and Palestinians.

One of the key strengths of the Confederation Model lies in its potential to address the concerns and aspirations of both sides without forcing either to relinquish its core identity. For Israel, the model preserves the Jewish character of the state while opening new avenues for cooperation with its Palestinian neighbors. For Palestine, it offers the prospect of sovereignty and self-determination without the restrictions that might come from a more traditional two-state arrangement, where borders and security concerns could still limit movement and economic development.

The shared institutions envisioned in the Confederation Model would play a crucial role in managing the complexities of this arrangement. These institutions would need to be carefully designed to balance the interests of both states, ensuring that neither feels overshadowed or marginalized. For example, a joint economic council could be established to coordinate economic policies, facilitate trade, and oversee shared infrastructure projects. This council could work to harmonize tax policies, labor regulations, and trade tariffs, making it easier for businesses to operate across borders and for people to work and live in either state. By fostering economic integration, the confederation could create a sense of shared prosperity that benefits both Israelis and Palestinians.

In the realm of security, the Confederation Model would require a high degree of cooperation and trust. Joint security operations, intelligence sharing, and coordinated responses to threats would be essential to maintaining stability. The establishment of a joint security council, with equal representation from both states, could help to ensure that security concerns are addressed in a balanced and effective manner. This council could oversee joint patrols in border areas, manage shared border crossings, and coordinate efforts to combat terrorism and other forms of violence. By working together on security, both states could enhance their own safety while building trust and reducing the likelihood of future conflicts.

The issue of Jerusalem, which has been one of the most contentious aspects of the Israel-Palestine conflict, could find a resolution within the Confederation Model. By designating Jerusalem as a shared capital, with joint administration and international oversight, the confederation could ensure that the city remains open and accessible to people of all faiths. This approach would preserve the city's unique cultural and religious significance while preventing it from becoming a flashpoint for further conflict. The joint council managing Jerusalem could be responsible for maintaining public order, protecting religious sites, and ensuring that the rights of all residents are respected.

The success of the Confederation Model would also depend on its ability to gain broad support from both populations. Public opinion would need to be swayed in favor of this new approach, which would require transparent communication and effective leadership. Both Israeli and Palestinian leaders would need to articulate the benefits of the confederation to their people, addressing fears and misconceptions while emphasizing the opportunities for peace and prosperity. This could involve a combination of public education campaigns, town hall meetings, and media outreach, designed to build consensus and generate enthusiasm for the confederation.

International support would be another critical factor in the success of the Confederation Model. The international community could provide crucial financial and technical assistance during the transition period, helping to establish the shared institutions and ensure that they operate smoothly. Diplomatic backing would also be essential, particularly in securing international guarantees for the confederation's security arrangements. Additionally, international organizations could play a role in monitoring the implementation of the confederation agreements, providing an impartial mechanism for resolving disputes and ensuring that both states adhere to their commitments.

One of the potential challenges of the Confederation Model is ensuring that the sovereignty of both states is respected. While the model calls for extensive cooperation, it must also allow each state to maintain its independence and national identity. This balance could be achieved through clear legal frameworks that delineate the powers of the shared institutions and the rights of each state. Both Israel and Palestine would need to retain control over their own domestic affairs, including education, healthcare, and cultural policies, while working together on issues of common interest. By striking this balance, the confederation could foster a sense of partnership without compromising the sovereignty of either state.

The economic dimension of the Confederation Model offers significant opportunities for growth and development. By pooling resources and coordinating economic policies, Israel and Palestine could create a more dynamic and integrated economy that benefits both sides. Joint infrastructure projects, such as roads, railways, and energy networks, could enhance connectivity and reduce costs, making it easier for goods and services to flow between the two states. Additionally, by aligning their economic policies, the two states could attract greater international investment, creating jobs and boosting economic growth.

Cultural exchange and social integration would also be important aspects of the Confederation Model. By encouraging greater interaction between Israelis and Palestinians, the confederation could help to build a sense of shared identity and mutual respect. This could involve joint educational programs, cultural festivals, and sports events that bring people together and foster a sense of community. Over time, these efforts could help to break down the barriers of mistrust and hostility, creating a more harmonious and peaceful society.

In conclusion, the Confederation Model offers a promising approach to resolving the Israel-Palestine conflict. By combining the advantages of sovereignty with the benefits of cooperation, it seeks to create a framework that allows both Israelis and Palestinians to achieve their national aspirations while living side by side in peace. While the challenges are significant, the potential rewards—a stable, prosperous, and peaceful region—make this model an option worth serious consideration. The success of the Confederation Model would depend on the willingness of both sides to embrace cooperation and mutual respect, as well as the support of the international community in facilitating the process. If implemented successfully, the Confederation Model could serve as a powerful example of how even the most intractable conflicts can be resolved through partnership, creativity, and a shared commitment to peace.

6

Comprehensive Peace Agreement

A Comprehensive Peace Agreement is a bold and ambitious approach to resolving the Israel-Palestine conflict by addressing all major issues in a single, overarching framework. The core idea behind such an agreement is to bring all relevant parties to the table, negotiate a deal that tackles the critical points of contention, and establish mechanisms to ensure that the agreement is both enforceable and sustainable over the long term. This chapter delves into the key components that would make a Comprehensive Peace Agreement effective and examines the challenges and opportunities associated with such an approach.

The involvement of all relevant parties is crucial to the success of a Comprehensive Peace Agreement. This includes not only Israel and the Palestinian Authority but also Hamas, neighboring Arab countries, and key international stakeholders. The inclusion of Hamas is particularly significant, given its influence in Gaza and its role as a major political and military force among Palestinians. While Hamas is considered a terrorist organization by many countries, its participation is essential for any agreement to be truly comprehensive and to ensure that the peace process has broad support among the Palestinian population. Similarly, neighboring Arab countries such as Egypt, Jordan, and Saudi Arabia, which have vested interests in the stability of the region, must be involved in the negotiations. These countries can act as guarantors of the agreement, providing political and economic support and helping to mediate between the parties. Additionally, key international stakeholders, including the United States, the European Union, Russia, and the United Nations, play a critical role in facilitating the negotiations, providing diplomatic backing, and offering economic incentives to encourage compliance with the agreement.

A Comprehensive Peace Agreement must be built on a detailed framework that addresses all major issues in the conflict. This framework should cover borders, security, the status of refugees, and the future of Jerusalem. The question of borders is particularly contentious, with the need to define the boundaries of a future Palestinian state and address the status of Israeli settlements in the West Bank. The agreement would need to establish clear, mutually agreed-upon borders, likely based on the pre-1967 lines with potential land swaps to accommodate both sides' concerns. Security arrangements would be another critical aspect, ensuring that both Israel and a future Palestinian state feel secure. This might involve the creation of a demilitarized zone, joint security patrols, or the deployment of international peacekeeping forces. The refugee issue would require a solution that balances the right of return for Palestinian refugees with the demographic and security concerns of Israel. Potential solutions could include compensation, resettlement in third countries, or limited return to the Palestinian state under certain conditions. The status of Jerusalem, a city of profound religious and cultural significance to both Israelis and Palestinians, would also need to be addressed. A possible solution could involve shared sovereignty, with East Jerusalem serving as the capital of Palestine and West Jerusalem as the capital of Israel, or a special international status for the city that guarantees access and rights for all.

For a Comprehensive Peace Agreement to be effective, it must be legally binding and supported by the international community. This means that the agreement should be enshrined in international law, with clear mechanisms for enforcement. These mechanisms could include international guarantees, such as security assurances provided by major powers or the United Nations, as well as economic incentives or sanctions to ensure compliance. The involvement of international actors in monitoring and verifying the implementation of the agreement would be essential to maintain trust and ensure that both sides adhere to their commitments.

Long-term monitoring and support are vital to the success of a Comprehensive Peace Agreement. The international community would need to establish a robust monitoring system to oversee the implementation of the agreement, detect violations, and address any issues that arise. This could involve the creation of an international monitoring body, composed of representatives from key stakeholders, tasked with regularly assessing progress and reporting to the international community. The monitoring body would have the authority to impose penalties for non-compliance, such as sanctions or other punitive measures, to ensure that both sides remain committed to the peace process. Additionally, international support in the form of financial aid, technical assistance, and capacity-building would be necessary to help the parties implement the agreement and build the institutions needed for long-term peace and stability.

The challenges of negotiating and implementing a Comprehensive Peace Agreement are significant. Bringing all relevant parties to the table and achieving consensus on the critical issues of borders, security, refugees, and Jerusalem will require immense diplomatic effort and compromise from all sides. The complexity of the issues involved, coupled with the deep-seated mistrust between Israelis and Palestinians, means that any agreement will need to be carefully crafted to address the concerns and aspirations of both peoples. Furthermore, the success of the agreement will depend on the willingness of the international community to provide ongoing support and oversight, ensuring that the agreement is implemented fully and fairly.

A Comprehensive Peace Agreement offers a pathway to resolving the Israel-Palestine conflict by addressing all major issues in a single, cohesive framework. By involving all relevant parties, establishing a detailed and legally binding framework, and setting up long-term monitoring and support mechanisms, such an agreement has the potential to bring about a lasting peace. However, the road to achieving this goal is fraught with challenges, and success will depend on the commitment of all parties involved, as well as the sustained engagement of the international community. If successful, a Comprehensive Peace Agreement could not only resolve the Israel-Palestine conflict but also serve as a model for resolving other complex and protracted conflicts around the world.

The potential of a Comprehensive Peace Agreement to resolve the Israel-Palestine conflict lies in its ability to address the root causes of the conflict and provide a structured pathway toward lasting peace. However, the complexity of such an agreement also requires a careful balancing of competing interests and the willingness of all parties to make significant compromises. For the agreement to be truly comprehensive, it must not only address the immediate issues but also lay the groundwork for a future where both Israelis and Palestinians can coexist peacefully and with mutual respect.

One of the critical aspects of a Comprehensive Peace Agreement is the creation of a viable Palestinian state. This state must be geographically contiguous, economically viable, and politically sovereign. The borders of this state would need to be clearly defined, taking into account the realities on the ground, including Israeli settlements in the West Bank. Land swaps could be used to accommodate the most significant settlements while ensuring that the Palestinian state has the territory it needs to function effectively. Additionally, the agreement must provide for the removal or integration of smaller settlements, ensuring that the Palestinian state is not fragmented into isolated enclaves. The establishment of secure and recognized borders would help to build trust between the two states and reduce the potential for future conflicts.

Security is another paramount concern in the Comprehensive Peace Agreement. Both Israel and a future Palestinian state must feel secure in their borders and confident that their sovereignty will be respected. To achieve this, the agreement could include provisions for joint security arrangements, such as coordinated patrols or shared intelligence, to prevent cross-border attacks and maintain peace. International peace-keeping forces could be deployed in sensitive areas, particularly along the borders, to act as a buffer and provide additional security. These forces could be mandated by the United Nations and would operate with the consent of both Israel and Palestine, ensuring that they are seen as neutral and impartial. The security framework must also address concerns about non-state actors, such as militant groups, by including measures to disarm these groups and integrate their members into civilian life through disarmament, demobilization, and reintegration programs.

The issue of Palestinian refugees is one of the most emotionally charged aspects of the conflict and will require a sensitive and pragmatic approach in the Comprehensive Peace Agreement. The right of return is a deeply held principle for many Palestinians, but it is also a significant concern for Israel, which fears that the mass return of refugees could undermine the Jewish character of the state. A potential solution could involve a combination of options: allowing a limited number of refugees to return to the Palestinian state, offering compensation for those who cannot return, and facilitating resettlement in third countries. International donors could play a crucial role in funding these compensation and resettlement programs, ensuring that they are implemented fairly and effectively. The goal would be to address the humanitarian needs of the refugees while preserving the demographic balance and security of both Israel and Palestine.

Jerusalem, as the spiritual and political heart of both nations, presents one of the most significant challenges in the peace process. Any solution must respect the religious and cultural significance of the city while also addressing the political aspirations of both Israelis and Palestinians. A shared sovereignty arrangement, where East Jerusalem serves as the capital of Palestine and West Jerusalem as the capital of Israel, could be a viable solution. Alternatively, Jerusalem could be given a special international status, with the city governed by a joint council of Israelis, Palestinians, and international representatives. This council would be responsible for maintaining public order, protecting religious sites, and ensuring that the rights of all residents are respected. Such an arrangement would need to guarantee access to the holy sites for people of all faiths, preserving the city's unique character as a center of religious significance.

The success of a Comprehensive Peace Agreement will also depend on the strength and enforceability of its legal framework. The agreement must be legally binding under international law, with clear mechanisms for enforcement and dispute resolution. This could involve the establishment of an international tribunal or arbitration panel to adjudicate any disputes that arise during the implementation of the agreement. The involvement of international guarantors—such as the United States, the European Union, Russia, and the United Nations—would provide additional assurance that the agreement will be upheld. These guarantors could offer security guarantees, economic incentives, and diplomatic support to both parties, ensuring that the agreement remains robust and durable.

Long-term monitoring and support are essential to ensure that the Comprehensive Peace Agreement is not just a temporary truce but a lasting solution. The international community would need to commit to ongoing involvement in the peace process, providing the necessary resources and expertise to help both Israel and Palestine implement the agreement. This could include funding for infrastructure projects, technical assistance for building effective governance institutions, and capacity-building programs for security forces. The international monitoring body would play a crucial role in overseeing the implementation of the agreement, detecting and addressing any violations, and providing regular reports to the international community. By maintaining a continuous presence and offering ongoing support, the international community can help to prevent the re-emergence of conflict and ensure that the peace process remains on track.

The challenges of achieving a Comprehensive Peace Agreement are undoubtedly significant. The deep-seated mistrust between Israelis and Palestinians, the complexity of the issues involved, and the influence of external actors all make the path to peace difficult. However, the potential rewards—a stable and peaceful Middle East, improved relations between Israel and the Arab world, and enhanced security for both Israelis and Palestinians—make the effort worthwhile. A successful Comprehensive Peace Agreement could serve as a model for resolving other protracted conflicts around the world, demonstrating that even the most intractable disputes can be overcome through negotiation, compromise, and international support.

A Comprehensive Peace Agreement offers a holistic approach to resolving the Israel-Palestine conflict, addressing all major issues in a single, cohesive framework. By involving all relevant parties, establishing a detailed and legally binding framework, and setting up long-term monitoring and support mechanisms, such an agreement has the potential to bring about a lasting peace. The road to achieving this goal is challenging, requiring the commitment of all parties involved and the sustained engagement of the international community. However, if successful, a Comprehensive Peace Agreement could transform the Israel-Palestine conflict from a seemingly intractable problem into a resolved issue, providing a foundation for peace, stability, and prosperity in the region for generations to come.

As with any major international agreement, the success of a Comprehensive Peace Agreement would depend on its ability to be adaptive and responsive to the evolving dynamics on the ground. The Middle East is a region marked by rapid changes, both politically and socially, and any peace agreement must be resilient enough to withstand shifts in leadership, public opinion, and external pressures. To this end, the Comprehensive Peace Agreement should include mechanisms for periodic review and adjustment, allowing the parties to revisit and renegotiate specific aspects of the agreement as circumstances change. These periodic reviews could be facilitated by an international body that oversees the implementation of the agreement, ensuring that any modifications are made transparently and with the consent of all parties involved.

One of the potential strengths of a Comprehensive Peace Agreement is its capacity to promote economic integration and cooperation between Israel and Palestine, which could serve as a stabilizing force for the region. By fostering economic interdependence, the agreement could create a situation where both sides have a vested interest in maintaining peace and stability. Joint economic initiatives, such as shared industrial zones, cross-border infrastructure projects, and collaborative research and development programs, could be central components of the peace agreement. These initiatives would not only provide tangible economic benefits but also help to build trust and reduce the animosities that have fueled the conflict for so long.

Involving neighboring Arab countries in the Comprehensive Peace Agreement is another critical factor for its success. The participation of key regional players like Egypt, Jordan, and Saudi Arabia could provide additional guarantees for the agreement and help to integrate Israel more fully into the broader Middle Eastern community. These countries could offer diplomatic support, security assurances, and economic partnerships that would reinforce the peace process. For example, Egypt and Jordan, both of which have peace treaties with Israel, could act as intermediaries to facilitate communication and resolve disputes between Israel and Palestine. Saudi Arabia, as a leading power in the Arab world, could help to mobilize broader Arab support for the agreement and provide financial backing for the economic initiatives outlined in the peace plan.

The role of the international community in supporting a Comprehensive Peace Agreement cannot be overstated. Beyond the initial negotiation and signing of the agreement, sustained international engagement will be necessary to ensure its long-term success. This includes providing the financial resources needed to implement the agreement, such as funding for infrastructure development, education, healthcare, and other vital services in the Palestinian territories. It also involves offering technical assistance to help build the institutions of a future Palestinian state, from a functioning judiciary and police force to effective governance and public administration. The international community can also play a key role in mediating any disputes that arise during the implementation phase, helping to prevent small issues from escalating into larger conflicts.

Education and public outreach are essential components of the Comprehensive Peace Agreement, as they help to ensure that the agreement is understood, accepted, and supported by the broader populations of both Israel and Palestine. Public awareness campaigns could be launched to explain the terms of the agreement, the benefits of peace, and the importance of cooperation between the two states. Educational initiatives could also focus on promoting tolerance, understanding, and reconciliation, helping to heal the deep wounds caused by decades of conflict. By fostering a culture of peace and cooperation, these efforts could help to ensure that the next generation of Israelis and Palestinians grows up with a mindset that supports coexistence rather than division.

The refugee issue, while one of the most challenging aspects of the conflict, also presents an opportunity for international cooperation and humanitarian action. The international community, working through agencies like the United Nations Relief and Works Agency (UNRWA) and other humanitarian organizations, could lead efforts to address the needs of Palestinian refugees. This could include providing compensation, facilitating resettlement, and supporting the reintegration of refugees into Palestinian society. A comprehensive solution to the refugee issue would not only address a major grievance of the Palestinian people but also contribute to the overall stability and sustainability of the peace agreement.

The enforcement mechanisms of the Comprehensive Peace Agreement must be robust and credible to ensure that both sides adhere to their commitments. This could involve the establishment of an international peacekeeping force, as well as the deployment of international observers to monitor compliance with the agreement. The peacekeeping force would be tasked with maintaining security in sensitive areas, such as the borders between Israel and Palestine, and ensuring that any violations of the agreement are promptly addressed. The observers, on the other hand, would report regularly on the progress of the agreement's implementation, providing transparency and accountability. In the event of a violation, the international community could impose sanctions or other punitive measures to compel compliance, ensuring that the peace process remains on track.

One of the ultimate goals of the Comprehensive Peace Agreement is to lay the foundation for a new era of relations between Israel and Palestine, one characterized by mutual respect, cooperation, and peaceful coexistence. This requires not only resolving the immediate issues at hand but also addressing the deeper, underlying causes of the conflict, such as historical grievances, identity, and narrative. To achieve this, the peace process must include initiatives aimed at fostering dialogue, reconciliation, and understanding between the two peoples. This could involve joint historical commissions to address contested narratives, truth and reconciliation commissions to address past injustices, and cultural exchange programs to build bridges between the two societies.

In conclusion, a Comprehensive Peace Agreement represents one of the most promising pathways to a sustainable and just resolution of the Israel-Palestine conflict. By addressing all major issues in a detailed and legally binding framework, involving all relevant parties, and setting up long-term monitoring and support mechanisms, such an agreement has the potential to bring about a lasting peace that benefits both Israelis and Palestinians. The challenges are immense, but with the commitment of the parties involved and the support of the international community, it is possible to overcome these obstacles and achieve a resolution that has eluded the region for so long. The success of the Comprehensive Peace Agreement could not only transform the lives of those directly affected by the conflict but also contribute to a more stable, peaceful, and prosperous Middle East, with positive implications for the entire world.

7

Economic Development and Integration

The chapter on Economic Development and Integration focuses on a crucial aspect of the Israel-Palestine peace process: the improvement of economic conditions for Palestinians. By enhancing economic opportunities and reducing poverty, the aim is to decrease tensions, foster stability, and create a vested interest in maintaining peace. Economic development is not only about boosting growth but also about addressing the underlying socio-economic disparities that fuel conflict and extremism. This chapter outlines the key components necessary to achieve meaningful economic development and integration between Israel and Palestine.

Investment in the Palestinian economy is the cornerstone of this approach. For sustainable peace to take root, there must be a concerted effort to build up the Palestinian economy, which has suffered from decades of conflict, occupation, and underdevelopment. International investment is critical in this regard, as it can provide the capital needed to develop infrastructure, enhance educational opportunities, and stimulate industrial growth. Infrastructure projects, such as building roads, improving water and energy supplies, and developing telecommunications, are essential for laying the groundwork for economic growth. Additionally, investing in education and vocational training can help to equip the Palestinian workforce with the skills needed to compete in the global economy. Industry development, particularly in sectors like manufacturing, agriculture, and technology, can create jobs, boost exports, and reduce reliance on foreign aid. International investors, including governments, development banks, and private sector entities, can play a significant role by providing the financial resources, expertise, and market access needed to support these initiatives.

Trade relations between Israel and Palestine are another critical component of economic integration. Facilitating trade between the two states can create economic interdependence, which, in turn, can serve as a stabilizing force in the region. By establishing a framework that encourages the free flow of goods, services, and people across borders, both economies can benefit from increased efficiency, lower costs, and expanded markets. For instance, Palestinian agricultural products could gain easier access to Israeli markets, while Israeli technology and expertise could help to modernize Palestinian industries. Joint ventures and partnerships between Israeli and Palestinian businesses could also be encouraged, fostering collaboration and mutual benefit. To facilitate this trade, it is essential to address the logistical and regulatory barriers that currently hinder cross-border commerce. This might involve harmonizing customs procedures, improving border infrastructure, and establishing joint trade commissions to oversee and promote economic cooperation. The goal is to create a seamless economic environment where both Israelis and Palestinians can prosper together, with trade serving as a bridge between the two communities.

Job creation is perhaps the most immediate and impactful way to improve economic conditions for Palestinians, particularly among the youth. High unemployment rates, especially among young Palestinians, have been a significant driver of social unrest and a recruiting ground for extremist groups. By creating jobs and providing meaningful employment opportunities, it is possible to mitigate the appeal of these groups and promote social stability. Job creation initiatives could focus on several key areas, including small and medium-sized enterprises (SMEs), public works projects, and entrepreneurship. SMEs are often the backbone of any economy, providing the majority of jobs and fostering innovation. Supporting the growth of Palestinian SMEs through access to finance, business development services, and market access can have a significant impact on employment. Public works projects, such as building schools, hospitals, and infrastructure, can provide immediate job opportunities while also improving public services. Encouraging entrepreneurship, particularly among young Palestinians, can help to unleash creativity and innovation, leading to the development of new industries and the creation of wealth. International organizations, donor countries, and the private sector can play a vital role in supporting these job creation efforts by providing funding, training, and access to markets.

In addition to these specific initiatives, broader economic policies and reforms will be necessary to create a conducive environment for economic development and integration. This includes ensuring the rule of law, protecting property rights, and creating a stable macroeconomic environment. Reforms in areas such as taxation, public finance management, and trade policy can help to attract investment and promote economic growth. Moreover, efforts to combat corruption and improve governance are essential to ensure that the benefits of economic development are widely shared and that public resources are used effectively. The international community can support these reforms by providing technical assistance, capacity building, and policy advice.

The success of economic development and integration efforts also depends on the broader political context. Economic initiatives must be closely linked to the peace process, with progress on the economic front reinforcing and being reinforced by progress on the political front. For example, as security improves and trust is built between the two sides, it may become possible to further liberalize trade, increase investment, and expand joint economic projects. Conversely, setbacks in the peace process could undermine economic gains, highlighting the need for a coordinated and holistic approach to peace building.

Economic development and integration are vital components of a comprehensive peace strategy between Israel and Palestine. By improving economic conditions for Palestinians, fostering trade relations, and creating jobs, it is possible to reduce tensions, promote stability, and create a vested interest in maintaining peace. These efforts require significant investment, international cooperation, and a supportive policy environment. However, the potential benefits—economic prosperity, social stability, and lasting peace—make these efforts essential. As economic ties between Israel and Palestine grow stronger, they can serve as a foundation for a more peaceful and cooperative future in the region.

To further enhance the impact of economic development and integration, it is essential to build robust economic institutions that can support sustained growth and development. These institutions would include financial systems, regulatory bodies, and public sector agencies that are capable of effectively managing the economy and ensuring that the benefits of growth are equitably distributed. Strengthening these institutions would involve capacity-building efforts, such as training government officials, improving financial oversight, and implementing transparent and accountable governance practices. A strong institutional framework is necessary to create a stable economic environment that can attract investment, foster innovation, and support the long-term development goals of the Palestinian economy.

One of the critical aspects of building these institutions is enhancing the financial sector in Palestine. A well-functioning financial sector is crucial for facilitating investment, enabling businesses to access credit, and supporting the growth of small and medium-sized enterprises (SMEs). Efforts to strengthen the banking system, develop capital markets, and promote financial inclusion can help to ensure that businesses and individuals have access to the financial services they need to thrive. This could involve providing technical assistance to Palestinian banks, encouraging partnerships with international financial institutions, and implementing regulatory reforms to improve the stability and efficiency of the financial sector. Additionally, promoting financial literacy and ensuring that marginalized groups, such as women and youth, have access to financial services can help to broaden the base of economic participation and reduce inequality.

Infrastructure development is another critical component of economic integration and development. Reliable infrastructure is the backbone of any economy, enabling the efficient movement of goods, services, and people. Investment in infrastructure, such as roads, ports, energy supply, and telecommunications, is essential for connecting Palestinian communities with each other and with the broader regional and global economy. These investments can help to reduce the cost of doing business, improve access to markets, and support the growth of key industries. Moreover, infrastructure projects can provide immediate employment opportunities, helping to address high levels of unemployment in Palestinian territories. International donors and development agencies can play a significant role in funding and implementing these infrastructure projects, working in partnership with Palestinian authorities to ensure that they meet the needs of the local population.

In the context of economic development and integration, education and workforce development are also vital. A well-educated and skilled workforce is necessary for driving innovation, improving productivity, and attracting investment. Efforts to improve the quality of education in Palestinian schools and universities, as well as to expand access to vocational training and higher education, are essential for preparing the next generation of Palestinians for the demands of the modern economy. These efforts could include curriculum reforms, teacher training programs, and the development of partnerships between educational institutions and the private sector to ensure that graduates have the skills needed by employers. Additionally, targeted programs to support women and marginalized groups in accessing education and training opportunities can help to ensure that the benefits of economic development are broadly shared and that all members of society have the opportunity to contribute to and benefit from economic growth.

International trade plays a crucial role in economic development, and fostering trade relations between Israel and Palestine is key to creating economic interdependence and stability. Facilitating the movement of goods and services across borders, reducing tariffs and non-tariff barriers, and improving customs procedures can help to increase trade flows and integrate the Palestinian economy with regional and global markets. Special attention should be given to sectors where Palestine has a comparative advantage, such as agriculture, tourism, and light manufacturing, to ensure that Palestinian products can compete effectively in international markets. Trade agreements and partnerships with neighboring countries and international trade organizations can further support the growth of Palestinian exports and create new opportunities for economic development.

Private sector development is another critical area of focus. A vibrant and dynamic private sector is essential for creating jobs, driving innovation, and sustaining economic growth. Encouraging entrepreneurship, particularly among Palestinian youth, can help to unleash creativity and foster the development of new industries. Programs that provide access to finance, mentorship, and business development services can support the growth of startups and SMEs, which are often the engines of job creation. Additionally, efforts to improve the business environment by reducing regulatory burdens, streamlining business registration processes, and combating corruption can help to attract investment and support the growth of the private sector.

Job creation, especially for Palestinian youth, is a priority that cannot be overstated. High unemployment rates, particularly among young people, contribute to social unrest and create an environment where extremist groups can thrive. By focusing on job creation, economic development efforts can address one of the root causes of conflict and contribute to long-term peace and stability. Public works programs, infrastructure projects, and initiatives to support SMEs and entrepreneurship can all contribute to job creation. Additionally, efforts to link education and training programs with labor market needs can ensure that young people have the skills and opportunities needed to secure employment and build a better future.

Regional cooperation is essential for the success of economic development and integration efforts. Working with neighboring countries, such as Jordan and Egypt, to develop cross-border infrastructure, harmonize trade policies, and promote regional economic integration can help to create a more stable and prosperous Middle East. Regional cooperation can also support the development of key sectors, such as energy and water management, that are vital for the long-term sustainability of the Palestinian economy. The international community can play a crucial role in facilitating this regional cooperation by providing funding, technical assistance, and diplomatic support.

Economic development and integration are essential components of a comprehensive peace strategy between Israel and Palestine. By investing in the Palestinian economy, fostering trade relations, creating jobs, and building strong institutions, it is possible to reduce tensions, promote stability, and create a vested interest in maintaining peace. These efforts require significant investment, international cooperation, and a supportive policy environment, but the potential benefits are immense. As economic ties between Israel and Palestine grow stronger, they can serve as a foundation for a more peaceful, stable, and prosperous future for both peoples, contributing to the broader goal of regional peace and stability.

To ensure the long-term success of economic development and integration between Israel and Palestine, it's crucial to embed these efforts within a broader framework of sustainable development. This involves not only focusing on immediate economic gains but also considering the environmental and social dimensions of development. Sustainable development can help create a resilient economy that benefits both current and future generations, ensuring that progress is not only achieved but also maintained over time.

One key aspect of this sustainable approach is the management of natural resources. Water, in particular, is a critical and often contentious resource in the region. Joint initiatives for water management can help ensure that both Israelis and Palestinians have access to clean, reliable water supplies, which is essential for agriculture, industry, and daily life. Cooperative water projects, such as desalination plants and wastewater treatment facilities, can be jointly developed and managed, promoting shared responsibility and mutual benefit. These projects can also serve as confidence-building measures, demonstrating the potential for collaboration even in areas of historical conflict.

Energy cooperation is another area where sustainable development can play a crucial role. By working together on renewable energy projects, such as solar and wind farms, Israel and Palestine can reduce their dependence on imported fuels, lower energy costs, and contribute to environmental sustainability. Joint energy projects can also create jobs and stimulate technological innovation, further contributing to economic growth. International donors and development organizations can support these efforts by providing funding, technical expertise, and facilitating partnerships between Israeli and Palestinian companies.

Agricultural development is another critical area where sustainable practices can yield significant benefits. Agriculture is a vital part of the Palestinian economy, and improving agricultural productivity can help to alleviate poverty, create jobs, and ensure food security. Sustainable farming practices, such as water-efficient irrigation, organic farming, and crop diversification, can enhance the resilience of Palestinian agriculture to climate change and other environmental challenges. Additionally, partnerships with Israeli agricultural companies and research institutions can facilitate the transfer of technology and knowledge, helping Palestinian farmers to improve yields and access new markets. International organizations can support these efforts by providing technical assistance, funding, and facilitating access to global agricultural markets.

Social sustainability is equally important in the context of economic development and integration. This involves ensuring that the benefits of economic growth are widely shared across society, reducing inequality and fostering social cohesion. Special attention should be given to marginalized groups, such as women, youth, and rural communities, to ensure that they have access to education, healthcare, and economic opportunities. Empowering these groups through targeted programs, such as microfinance initiatives, vocational training, and entrepreneurship support, can help to build a more inclusive and equitable economy. Social protection measures, such as unemployment benefits, health insurance, and pensions, can also play a role in reducing poverty and vulnerability, ensuring that all members of society can benefit from economic progress.

The role of civil society in promoting sustainable development and integration cannot be overlooked. Non-governmental organizations (NGOs), community groups, and other civil society organizations can play a vital role in advocating for sustainable development practices, holding governments accountable, and ensuring that the voices of all stakeholders are heard. These organizations can also facilitate dialogue and cooperation between Israeli and Palestinian communities, helping to build trust and understanding at the grassroots level. International donors can support the work of civil society by providing funding, capacity-building, and platforms for collaboration.

Another important aspect of sustainable development is the preservation of cultural heritage and the promotion of cultural exchange. The Israel-Palestine region is rich in cultural and historical heritage, which can be leveraged to promote tourism, create jobs, and foster a sense of shared identity. Joint initiatives to preserve cultural sites, promote cultural festivals, and encourage cultural exchange can help to build bridges between Israeli and Palestinian communities, reducing tensions and promoting mutual respect. Tourism, in particular, has the potential to become a significant source of income for both economies, as well as a means of showcasing the region's rich cultural diversity to the world. International organizations, such as UNESCO, can play a role in supporting these efforts by providing expertise, funding, and facilitating international cultural exchange programs.

Environmental sustainability is also a key consideration in the context of economic development and integration. Efforts to promote green technologies, reduce carbon emissions, and protect natural habitats can help to ensure that economic growth does not come at the expense of the environment. Joint environmental projects, such as reforestation, wildlife conservation, and pollution control, can also serve as confidence-building measures, demonstrating the potential for cooperation in addressing common challenges. International donors and environmental organizations can support these efforts by providing funding, technical assistance, and facilitating partnerships between Israeli and Palestinian environmental groups.

In conclusion, sustainable development is a critical component of the broader strategy for economic development and integration between Israel and Palestine. By focusing on the long-term sustainability of economic growth, natural resource management, social inclusion, cultural preservation, and environmental protection, it is possible to create a resilient economy that benefits both current and future generations. These efforts require significant investment, international cooperation, and a supportive policy environment, but the potential benefits are immense. As Israel and Palestine work together to build a sustainable and integrated economy, they can lay the foundation for a more peaceful, stable, and prosperous future, not only for themselves but for the entire region.

8

Cultural and Religious Reconciliation

The chapter on Cultural and Religious Reconciliation addresses one of the most profound and challenging aspects of the Israel-Palestine conflict: the deep-seated cultural and religious tensions that have persisted for decades. These tensions are rooted in the historical narratives, religious beliefs, and cultural identities of the people involved, making them difficult to resolve through political agreements alone. To build a lasting peace, it is essential to address these issues directly through dialogue, reconciliation, and mutual understanding. This chapter explores the key components necessary for fostering cultural and religious reconciliation between Israelis and Palestinians.

Interfaith dialogue is a critical element in promoting understanding and respect among the Jewish, Muslim, and Christian communities in the region. Given the central role that religion plays in the identities of both Israelis and Palestinians, fostering dialogue between religious leaders and communities is essential for breaking down barriers and dispelling misconceptions. Interfaith dialogue provides a platform for members of different religious communities to come together, share their beliefs, and discuss their differences in a respectful and constructive manner. These dialogues can help to humanize the "other" by allowing individuals to see beyond stereotypes and recognize the shared values and common humanity that exist across religious divides. Religious leaders, in particular, can play a vital role in these efforts by advocating for peace, tolerance, and coexistence within their own communities. Moreover, interfaith dialogue can serve as a powerful tool for addressing the religious aspects of the conflict, such as the status of Jerusalem and access to holy sites, by fostering a spirit of compromise and mutual respect.

Cultural exchanges are another important avenue for building mutual respect and understanding between Israelis and Palestinians. Cultural exchanges involve the sharing of artistic, literary, musical, and other cultural expressions between communities, allowing individuals to experience and appreciate each other's traditions, histories, and perspectives. These exchanges can take many forms, including joint cultural festivals, art exhibits, music performances, and literary collaborations. By participating in each other's cultural events, Israelis and Palestinians can develop a deeper appreciation for the richness and diversity of their respective cultures. Cultural exchanges also provide an opportunity for creative collaboration, where artists, writers, and musicians from both sides can work together to produce works that reflect their shared experiences and aspirations. These collaborative efforts can serve as a bridge between communities, fostering a sense of shared identity and common purpose. In addition to formal cultural exchanges, informal interactions between individuals—such as visits to each other's homes, participation in community events, and shared meals—can also play a significant role in breaking down cultural barriers and building personal connections.

Addressing historical narratives is perhaps the most challenging but also the most essential component of cultural and religious reconciliation. The conflict between Israelis and Palestinians is deeply intertwined with competing historical narratives, each of which is rooted in a sense of victimhood and righteousness. For Israelis, the narrative often centers on the historical persecution of Jews, the Holocaust, and the establishment of Israel as a safe haven for the Jewish people. For Palestinians, the narrative is shaped by the experience of displacement, occupation, and the struggle for national self-determination. These narratives are not just stories of the past; they are integral to the identities of both peoples and have a powerful influence on how they perceive the conflict and each other. To move toward reconciliation, it is necessary to engage in a process of historical dialogue that acknowledges the suffering and aspirations of both sides. This process might involve the creation of joint historical commissions, where historians, educators, and community leaders from both sides come together to examine and discuss their respective histories. The goal of these commissions would not be to impose a single, unified narrative, but rather to create a space where multiple perspectives can be heard and respected. Through this process, it may be possible to identify shared historical experiences and values that can serve as a foundation for a more inclusive and empathetic understanding of the past.

In addition to these formal efforts, education plays a crucial role in cultural and religious reconciliation. Educational curricula in both Israel and Palestine should be reviewed and revised to ensure that they promote a balanced and respectful understanding of the other side's history, culture, and religion. This might involve the inclusion of materials that highlight the contributions of different communities to the region's cultural and religious heritage, as well as the use of textbooks and teaching methods that encourage critical thinking and empathy. Schools can also serve as venues for interfaith and intercultural activities, where students from different backgrounds can learn and interact with each other in a positive and supportive environment. By fostering a culture of tolerance and mutual respect from a young age, education can help to lay the groundwork for a future in which Israelis and Palestinians can coexist peacefully.

Media and communication also have a significant role to play in cultural and religious reconciliation. The media can be a powerful tool for shaping public perceptions and attitudes, and it is essential that it is used responsibly to promote understanding and dialogue rather than perpetuate stereotypes and hatred. Efforts should be made to encourage balanced and fair reporting on issues related to the conflict, as well as to highlight stories of cooperation, coexistence, and shared experiences between Israelis and Palestinians. Social media platforms can also be used to facilitate dialogue and connection between individuals from different communities, providing a space for conversations that might not be possible in more traditional settings.

The role of international actors in supporting cultural and religious reconciliation is also important. International organizations, NGOs, and governments can provide funding, expertise, and platforms for dialogue and exchange initiatives. They can also help to facilitate the involvement of global religious and cultural leaders, who can bring additional perspectives and support to the reconciliation process. Furthermore, international actors can use their influence to encourage political leaders on both sides to prioritize reconciliation efforts as part of the broader peace process.

Cultural and religious reconciliation is a vital component of any comprehensive peace strategy between Israel and Palestine. By addressing the deep-seated cultural and religious tensions that underpin the conflict through interfaith dialogue, cultural exchanges, and the re-examination of historical narratives, it is possible to build a foundation for lasting peace and coexistence. These efforts require the commitment of individuals and communities on both sides, as well as the support of international actors, to create an environment where understanding, respect, and empathy can flourish. While the challenges are significant, the potential rewards—peace, reconciliation, and a shared future—make these efforts essential.

To further enhance the effectiveness of cultural and religious reconciliation, it is essential to integrate these initiatives into the broader peace process, ensuring that they complement and reinforce political and economic efforts to resolve the conflict. Reconciliation cannot be achieved in isolation; it must be part of a comprehensive strategy that addresses the underlying causes of the conflict, including issues of land, sovereignty, security, and refugees. By embedding cultural and religious reconciliation within the larger framework of peacebuilding, it becomes possible to create a more holistic and sustainable path to peace.

One way to achieve this integration is through the establishment of joint Israeli-Palestinian committees or councils dedicated to promoting reconciliation. These bodies could be composed of representatives from various sectors, including religious leaders, educators, cultural figures, and civil society organizations. The committees would be tasked with developing and implementing programs that foster dialogue, cultural exchange, and mutual understanding between the two communities. They could also serve as advisory bodies to the political leadership, providing input on how reconciliation initiatives can be aligned with ongoing peace negotiations. By institutionalizing reconciliation efforts, these committees can help to ensure that they receive the necessary resources and attention and that they are coordinated with other aspects of the peace process.

Another important aspect of reconciliation is the creation of safe spaces where individuals from different communities can come together to engage in dialogue and build relationships. These spaces could take the form of community centers, dialogue forums, or online platforms, where people can share their experiences, discuss sensitive issues, and explore common ground. The emphasis in these spaces should be on listening, empathy, and mutual respect, rather than on trying to reach immediate agreements or resolve all differences. The goal is to create an environment where people feel comfortable expressing their views and where they can begin to see each other as partners in the pursuit of peace, rather than as adversaries.

The arts can also play a powerful role in cultural and religious reconciliation. Artistic expressions, such as theater, film, music, and visual arts, can transcend language and cultural barriers, allowing people to connect on a deeper emotional level. Collaborative artistic projects that involve Israeli and Palestinian artists working together can serve as a metaphor for the larger reconciliation process, demonstrating that it is possible to create something beautiful and meaningful through cooperation. These projects can also provide a platform for exploring difficult issues, such as the impact of the conflict on individuals and communities, in a way that is accessible and engaging. Art has the unique ability to evoke empathy and to help people see the world from perspectives other than their own, making it an invaluable tool for reconciliation.

Storytelling is another powerful medium for reconciliation. By sharing personal stories of loss, hope, and resilience, individuals from both sides can humanize the conflict and foster a deeper understanding of each other's experiences. Storytelling initiatives can take many forms, from oral history projects and documentary films to written memoirs and digital storytelling platforms. These initiatives can provide a voice to those who have been marginalized or silenced by the conflict, allowing their stories to be heard and acknowledged. In doing so, storytelling can help to build bridges between communities and to create a shared narrative that recognizes the suffering and aspirations of all those affected by the conflict.

Religious reconciliation efforts can also be supported by joint religious initiatives, such as interfaith prayer services, pilgrimages, and study groups. These initiatives can provide opportunities for members of different faiths to come together in a spirit of humility and reverence, focusing on their shared values and spiritual connections. Religious leaders can play a key role in these efforts by advocating for peace and reconciliation within their congregations and by using their influence to promote tolerance and understanding. Joint religious initiatives can also address specific issues related to the conflict, such as the status of holy sites, by fostering dialogue and cooperation between the relevant religious communities.

The importance of involving youth in reconciliation efforts cannot be overstated. Young people are often the most affected by the conflict, yet they also have the greatest potential to drive change and to build a future based on peace and cooperation. Youth-focused reconciliation programs, such as leadership training, peace education, and intercultural exchange programs, can empower young Israelis and Palestinians to become leaders in the reconciliation process. These programs can also help to break the cycle of violence by providing young people with the skills and opportunities to resolve conflicts peacefully and to engage in constructive dialogue with their peers from the other side. By investing in the next generation, it is possible to build a more resilient and peaceful society.

Education, in general, plays a critical role in shaping the attitudes and beliefs of future generations. Integrating peace education into school curricula is essential for fostering a culture of reconciliation and coexistence. This could involve teaching about the history and cultures of both Israelis and Palestinians, promoting critical thinking and empathy, and encouraging students to engage in dialogue and conflict resolution. Schools can also be places where students from different backgrounds come together to learn and interact, helping to break down the barriers of fear and mistrust that have been built up over decades of conflict. Teachers and educators have a vital role to play in this process, and they should be provided with the training and resources needed to effectively teach about peace and reconciliation.

To ensure the long-term success of cultural and religious reconciliation efforts, it is important to establish mechanisms for monitoring and evaluating their impact. This could involve regular assessments of reconciliation programs, surveys of public attitudes, and the collection of data on intercommunal relations. By tracking progress and identifying areas where additional efforts are needed, it is possible to continuously improve reconciliation initiatives and to ensure that they are meeting their goals. International organizations, academic institutions, and civil society organizations can play a key role in supporting these monitoring and evaluation efforts, providing expertise, resources, and platforms for sharing best practices.

Finally, it is important to recognize that reconciliation is a long-term process that requires patience, persistence, and commitment. The wounds of the Israel-Palestine conflict run deep, and healing them will take time. However, by fostering dialogue, cultural exchange, and a shared understanding of history, it is possible to build a foundation for lasting peace. These efforts must be sustained and supported by all levels of society, from political leaders to grassroots organizations, and must be seen as an integral part of the broader peace process. While the road to reconciliation may be challenging, the potential rewards—a future where Israelis and Palestinians can live together in peace and mutual respect—make the journey worthwhile.

9

Building a Future of Peace

The concluding chapter of this book brings together the various approaches, strategies, and solutions discussed throughout the text to offer a comprehensive vision for a peaceful resolution to the Israel-Palestine conflict. The journey toward peace is complex, fraught with deep-seated challenges, but it is also filled with opportunities for transformation and hope. This chapter reflects on the key insights gained from exploring the conflict from multiple angles—political, economic, cultural, and religious—and emphasizes the necessity of a multifaceted approach to achieving lasting peace.

Throughout this book, we have explored the importance of addressing the root causes of the conflict, from historical grievances and territorial disputes to economic disparities and cultural tensions. We have examined the potential of various solutions, such as the Two-State Solution, the One-State Solution, and the Confederation Model, each offering a unique pathway to peace. We have also considered the critical role of international intervention, economic development, and cultural reconciliation in supporting these political frameworks.

At the heart of these discussions is the recognition that peace cannot be achieved through political agreements alone. While such agreements are essential for establishing the legal and structural foundations of peace, they must be accompanied by efforts to address the deeper social, economic, and cultural dimensions of the conflict. This includes fostering economic development and integration to improve living conditions and reduce tensions, promoting cultural and religious reconciliation to build mutual understanding and respect, and involving the international community to provide the necessary support and oversight.

The concept of reconciliation, both political and social, is a recurring theme in this book. Reconciliation requires acknowledging the pain and suffering experienced by both Israelis and Palestinians, recognizing each other's legitimate aspirations, and committing to a future where both peoples can coexist in peace and security. It involves difficult conversations, compromises, and the willingness to move beyond past grievances toward a shared future. Reconciliation is not a one-time event but an ongoing process that must be nurtured and supported over time.

The importance of leadership in this process cannot be overstated. Political leaders on both sides must have the vision and courage to pursue peace, even in the face of opposition and setbacks. They must be willing to take bold steps to reach out to the other side, build trust, and create an environment conducive to dialogue and cooperation. However, leadership is not limited to politicians; it also includes religious leaders, community leaders, and civil society actors who can play a crucial role in shaping public opinion and promoting reconciliation at the grassroots level.

One of the most significant lessons from this exploration is the power of collaboration and partnership. Peace cannot be imposed from the outside; it must be built from within, through the active participation of both Israelis and Palestinians. International actors can support this process by providing resources, expertise, and diplomatic backing, but the primary responsibility for peace rests with the people who live in the region. This means that any viable solution must be inclusive, taking into account the needs and perspectives of all stakeholders, including those who have been marginalized or excluded from the peace process in the past.

The path to peace is neither easy nor straightforward, but it is achievable if both sides are willing to engage in good faith and work toward a common goal. The process will require patience, persistence, and a commitment to dialogue and cooperation. There will undoubtedly be challenges and setbacks along the way, but these should be seen not as insurmountable obstacles, but as opportunities to learn, adapt, and continue moving forward.

As we conclude this book, it is important to remember that peace is not just the absence of conflict; it is the presence of justice, equality, and mutual respect. It is about creating a future where both Israelis and Palestinians can live in dignity, with their rights protected and their aspirations fulfilled. This vision of peace is not only desirable but necessary for the stability and prosperity of the entire region.

In closing, the journey toward peace in Israel and Palestine is one that requires the collective efforts of all—leaders, citizens, and the international community. It is a journey that demands both courage and compassion, as well as a deep commitment to the values of justice and human dignity. While the road ahead may be long and difficult, the potential rewards—a future of peace, security, and coexistence for Israelis and Palestinians—make the journey well worth taking. Let us hope that the insights and strategies discussed in this book can contribute to a future where peace is not just a possibility, but a reality.